We Believe in Miracles

by

L. Paul and Alice Prather

We Believe in Miracles,
by L. Paul and Alice Prather

ISBN # 0-89228-002-6

Published for L. Paul and Alice Prather, by
Impact Christian Books, Inc.
332 Leffingwell, Suite 101,
Kirkwood, Missouri 63122
314-822-3309

Printed in the United States of America

TABLE OF CONTENTS

ACKNOWLEDGMENTS

Many people have helped us in one way or another and we feel a deep appreciation for each one. A special thanks to the following:

Paul D. Prather, our son, for editing and for encouragement.

Cathi Toy, our daughter, for computer help, for faith in us, and her optimism.

Mary Jo Whitaker for her encouragement and her optimism about getting the book published and **Bobby Joe Whitaker**, posthumously, for reading the book and for his encouragement.

Missy Gibson for reading and correcting the manuscript, and for encouragement.

Bee Gibson for her encouragement.

Members of Faith Church for their prayers, encouragement, and financial help in getting the book published.

John Krebs for help in many ways.

Those who have been involved in the miracles.

Most of all to God, for His never ending blessings. Without Him there would be no miracles to write about.

i

PREFACE
by Alice

Paul and I have not written this book in order to boast of anything we may, or may not, have done. We have written this to boast of a loving, caring God.

If we can somehow call attention to how God cares for all of us and if we can make you aware of how God is at work in your life, then you can boast of Him, too. You may be saying, "that was luck," or "what a coincidence," when it has been a loving God at work in your life all the time. If we can teach you to give credit where credit is due, then our work has not been in vain.

We have used our own family member's names but where other people are concerned, we have not given their specific names.

A few of the accounts have been told twice. Once as I saw it and once as Paul saw it.

As you read this, remember we still stand in awe at what God has done and how He has chosen to do it. As you think back on your own life, remember it has been said, God works in mysterious ways, His wonders to perform.

May God bless you.

INTRODUCTION
by Paul

Mark 16:17--- *"These signs shall follow those who believe . . . "*

The denomination in which we were reared taught that signs and wonders stopped when the original disciples died. We were taught that unusual things did sometimes happen but they were mostly coincidences. Miracles passed away when the New Testament age closed.

When I began to read the Bible for myself rather than listen to someone else, I could find nothing which indicated that signs and wonders ceased when Jesus and his original disciples were gone. Rather, I found that the promises of God were for today, too.

Then, I began to read some books which gave accounts of modern day miracles. One day a thought struck me: if parts of the Bible are not for today, perhaps none of it is. I began to seriously seek the truth. Slowly, I began to see little miracles happen. Then, the big one happened to me---I was baptized in the Holy Spirit. A few months later I was healed of cancer. Other things for which there was no logical explanation happened. God seemed to be showing me very deliberately, very slowly that He is God and He is still at work.

The examples Alice and I share with you in this book are experiences in which we have been personally involved. In order to protect the privacy of the people involved, we have not given specific names or places.

These stories are being told to point people to the God,

El Shaddai, who is more than enough "*to meet all our needs according to His riches in glory through Christ Jesus.*" (Phil. 4:19) We seek no glory or honor for any of these miracles. We give all glory and honor to Him.

We do not feel that we are special. Whatever is available to us is available to all who believe. God's basic order for miracles is ask, believe, and receive.

I pray for you as you read about these miracles. I pray that you may see Him and the power of His Glory.

In order to set the stage for all the other miracles we write about, I thought it important to share with you first what I consider the miracles of all miracles:

THE GREATEST MIRACLE OF ALL
by Paul

The greatest miracle of all is to be born again---the miracle of salvation.

The church in which I was reared believed a person just could not get saved unless he went to the mourner's bench which was normally the front pew. It was called the "mourner's bench" because people went there to weep and mourn over their sins until God heard them and forgave them.

When I was about eleven or twelve years old, during a very highly emotional revival meeting, I told my mother I wanted to go to the mourners bench and "get saved." Many people were kneeling there trying to "pray through." There were also 'personal workers' kneeling beside them to help them pray. Two of these workers knelt beside me. On one side of me, one was saying to me, "Just *turn loose* and let Jesus save you!" On the other side, someone else was saying, "Just *hang on* and Jesus will save you!" I didn't know whether to turn loose or hang on. Finally, one of the men said to me, "Just stand up and receive Jesus as your Savior!" I stood up and said something like, "I receive Jesus Christ as my Lord and Savior!" When I did, something wonderful happened inside me. I was aware of a new Power living in me. On that day I became a child of God. A miracle had happened---I had become a "new creature in Christ Jesus." (II Cor. 5:17). I started walking with the Lord that day and I have been walking with Him for more than fifty years. A miracle had happened.

In a few years I gave my entire life to Jesus and yielded myself to doing His will. Thinking at the time a person could only serve the Lord by preaching or being a missionary, I surrendered my life to become a preacher when I was nineteen years old. I enrolled in school to prepare myself for the ministry.

Several years later, I became a pastor in a very evangelistic denomination. I caught the fire of being a 'soul winner.' I prayed fervently for God to use me to lead people to know Him as their Lord.

In the late 1960s and early 1970s my position required me to travel a great deal. Before each trip I asked God to put someone on the highway hitch hiking to whom I could witness. Once, I was on a fairly deserted back road after I had prayed this prayer. Soon, I came up on one of those little knolls in the road and there stood a man trying to hitch a ride. Something inside me said. "There's your man. He is the answer to your prayer!" Soon after I had stopped to pick him up and he had gotten into my car, I asked him if he was a Christian. He replied that he was not and I asked him if he wanted to be saved. He said, "I am just going to Science Hill. I don't have time to get saved." I started driving very slowly and telling him about Jesus. In a few minutes, I pulled off the road into a church parking lot and prayed with him. He received Jesus as his Savior and we both went on our ways rejoicing.

On another day, I prayed simply, "Lord let me lead someone to Jesus today." In a short time, I noticed my gas gauge was showing almost empty. I pulled into the first gasoline station I reached. One of the attendants came out to put gas in for me and I went in the station. There was a young man in the station attending the cash register. I introduced myself and invited him to revival services where

I was preaching a few miles away. Next, I asked him if he was a Christian. He replied, "No, I am not but I want to be! I have been praying all day for God to send me someone to tell me how to get saved!" Before the other attendant returned to the station, he had accepted Jesus as his Lord and Savior. Again, I went on my way rejoicing!

There was a very dedicated young woman who was a faithful member of one church of which I was pastor. She brought her children to every meeting of the church and always said, "Pray for Robert to be saved." Robert was an alcoholic and a bootlegger. They lived in a little shanty on the side of a one lane dirt road. One time when I went to visit them I heard weird noises in the walls and attic. She said, "Oh, pastor, don't mind that noise, it's just the rats playing!" She was serious---it was the rats playing! When I would go to visit them, I would go in the front door and Robert would go out the back door.

One day, I heard that Robert was laying stone for a fireplace in a new house which was being built. When I caught up with him there and began to talk to him about Jesus, this big, muscular, hunk of a man began to cry very loudly. He was making so much noise crying I could hardly understand him when he spoke. But after we had gotten down on our knees in that dirty room, I could hear him pray, out loud, not caring who heard him, "Lord, I am sorry for my sins. Forgive me of my sins and save me right now!" Then, a big smile came on his face and the crying stopped. He came to church that night and publicly confessed Jesus as his Lord. Several years later he was ordained a deacon and then later moved to Indiana where he helped start a church. Believe me, this was a miracle.

I was pastor of a church in a community where most people attended church, members or not. One of those who attended was a fine man whose wife and children were members but he was not a Christian. I prayed for him often. One day as I was praying for him, I felt the still small voice within me say, "This is John's day of salvation. Go and introduce him to Jesus." I immediately quit praying and went to his house. No one was home. I went back several times that day and still no one was home. I knew that he normally went to work at 2:30, so when I looked at my watch at 2:00, I started for his house one last time and arrived about 2:10. When I went in and told him I wanted to talk to him, he reminded me that he went to work at 2:30. I said, "John, the Lord told me this was your day of salvation and I have come to talk you about Jesus." I quickly read the Scripture and prayed with him. He received Jesus as his Savior and I went on my way at 2:20. He joined the church, was baptized, and became an 'on fire' Christian. Later, he was chosen to become a trustee.

These stories are not about me going to witness---they are about Jesus performing miracles in the lives of people, changing people who needed to be changed, and giving them life eternal.

If you don't know Him in your heart as your Savior, please pray this prayer (or something similar): "Dear Lord, I know I am a sinner. Please forgive me of my sins and come to live in my heart. I accept you as my Lord and Savior right now. Thank you, Jesus, for saving me."

"...if you confess with your mouth Jesus as Lord, and believe in your heart that God has raised Him from the dead, you shall be saved; for with the heart man believes, resulting in righteousness, and with the mouth he confesses resulting in salvation."

(Romans 10:9-10)

SECTION 1

HEALING MIRACLES

CANCER IS HEALED
by Paul

One day in late December 1975, I was lying in the floor listening to the radio. When I turned over, I discovered a large knot on the top of my head, as if I had been hit or had bumped my head some way. While I watched the knot for a few days, a great deal of pain began going down the right side of my head and into my neck. Eventually, when the knot did not go away, I went to see my family doctor. He sent me to the hospital for x-rays and discovered what appeared to be a 'Venus lake' which is a pool of blood. After other examinations, it became apparent that the problem was a small tumor. My doctor sent me to Lexington to see a specialist. In a few days, I was admitted to a hospital.

In the hospital, doctors found a tumor between the layers of my skull and a larger tumor in my kidney. The doctors were sure the tumor in my head was a metastatic tumor feeding off the tumor in my kidney. They were sure it was malignant.

The word cancer, or malignancy, is a very traumatic word to hear when it refers to your own body. At first I thought, "My life is over!" Thoughts about the pain of leaving my wife and children and all of my unfinished business possessed me. I panicked at the thought of dying.

A series of events allowed me to go home for part of Saturday and Sunday before surgery was scheduled. While I was home, I went to our church and asked them to anoint me with oil and pray for my healing in the name of Jesus. I went back to the hospital assured of being healed. After all, I had done what God told me in His Word to do. Now, all I had to do was wait for Him to fulfill His promise. Many people who came to see me encouraged me with such words as, "I just know you are going to be healed."

On Monday they took a biopsy of the tumor in my head and the tests showed it to be a high-grade malignancy. After a battery of other tests, we were told I had cancer all over my body, and bone tissue taken from any part of my body would be malignant. The report had one encouraging aspect; it was the fast kind of cancer. I would be dead in a short time--two to six months, with an outside chance of living for as much as five years. However, since I was also a diabetic, the possibility of living that long was very remote.

A decision was made to start me on chemotherapy on Wednesday. The day my treatment was to begin the doctor came in and said, "That report has completely changed. While the pathologist was studying the tissue, it became less malignant as each slide came through and he has concluded that the malignancy is gone." We were ecstatic, but had to wait on another report from the kidney specialist. He reported the tumor there had disappeared. We concluded I was healed.

Alice got on the phone to call everyone we knew who cared and exclaimed, "He's healed! He's healed! Praise the Lord. He's healed!" Further tests showed the cancer was gone. That was 19 years ago and I am still healed today.

"He (Jesus) Himself bore our sins in His body on the cross, that we might die to sin and live to righteousness; for by His stripes you are healed." (I Peter 2:24)

4

OUR CHILDREN ARE MIRACLES
by Paul

After Alice and I had been married for about two years, we decided to start a family. It didn't happen the way it was supposed to happen.

First, we learned that Alice had a physical condition which would, in all probability, keep her from ever becoming pregnant. In those days we did not know God could and would perform miracles, but we believed in prayer. Don't ask me how we reconciled these contradictions because I do not know the answer. However, we began to say to God, "If you will give us a son, we will give him back to you."

Sometime after we began to pray this prayer, Alice became quite ill. It seemed she had some kind of stomach problem accompanied by pain and some swelling. I persuaded her to go to the doctor because I thought she had a tumor. I was fully persuaded she would have to go into the hospital for surgery. Our family doctor, who knew we wanted children, examined her thoroughly and said, "I believe this is the kind of tumor you want--you're pregnant!" When we got out of the office and into the hallway, we began to jump, squeal, and shout praises to the Lord. We knew He had heard our prayer and answered us. He had kept His part of the bargain, so we tried to the best of our ability to keep ours.

The first Sunday after our son was born, we took him to church and publicly dedicated him to the Lord. We tried to teach him the things of God and live a Christian life before him. Now, he is serving the Lord as a pastor, writer, and dedicated father and husband.

In the early months of 1960, we discovered Alice was pregnant again. We were elated. She carried the baby about two weeks over the normal nine months and could not go into labor. Finally, she had a Caesarean and the baby was born dead. We didn't know why this happened, and still don't, but we know God "causes all things to work together for our good" and for His glory when we trust Him.

A year or more after this happened, Alice was reading our Kentucky denomination's paper and saw an article about the child-care program having children for adoption. We decided to write and see if we could adopt a baby. They called us for an interview and explained that there were 24 couples ahead of us. We didn't really want to be selfish, but we asked God to have them skip over those other couples and give us a child. They asked us if we wanted a boy or a girl. We answered, "A baby!" They asked us if we would take twins or triplets. We told them, "Yes." They asked us why we wanted another child. We simply answered, "To love."

We passed all those tests with high marks. However, there was one area in which we were sure to fail--finances. We were dirt poor in earthly goods, while we were rich in a vision of good things to come. We evidently had what they were looking for: potential. They checked us out thoroughly because they thought Alice matched the birth mother perfectly.

One day when we were least expecting it, a social worker called Alice at work and told her they had a baby girl for us. We were to pick her up the next day. We had made no preparations because they had told us it might be two years before a baby would be available. She called me at the school where I was substitute teaching to tell me to come home and get ready to go get our new daughter. Some legal question came up at the last minute to postpone the blessed event for another week. That was one of the longest weeks we ever spent.

Cathi was 15 days old when we brought her home. We were the proud parents of a chubby, beautiful little girl. We gave her back to the Lord and dedicated her to Him on the first Sunday after we brought her home. She was born for us. She was, and is, ours. We have never known any difference between the one who was born to us through Alice's body and the one who was born to us through another woman's body. Cathi is active in the church, has been to Mexico on a missionary journey, and is a blessing to all those around her. She is our miracle girl. God smiled on us and gave us two wonderful children.

We learned God hears our prayers and answers them in His way----not ours. His ways are always better than ours.

"'For My thoughts are not your thoughts, neither are your ways My ways,' declares the Lord. 'For as the heavens are higher than the earth, so are My ways higher than your ways, and My thoughts higher than your thoughts.' "

(Isaiah 55:8-9)

THE MIRACLE OF A BABY BOY--OURS!
by Alice

I hadn't been the least bit interested in marrying a preacher. I didn't have many role models to choose from but from the ones I had, I was sure being a pastor's wife definitely wasn't for me. Since I was so young, clothes, pretty hair, dating, going places and having good times were my main interests. Being a quiet, sad-looking woman with a houseful of children was not what I had in mind.

However, there was one catch to all this: I really liked the preacher a lot. He was a silver- tongued orator, too. He tore down all my reasons why I thought I couldn't possibly be a preacher's wife. He said he wouldn't expect me to wear my hair in a bun and have a lot of children. He won and we were married a few months later.

A year or two passed and I began to get that I-want-to-be-a-mother feeling--really bad! There was only one problem--it didn't happen and the doctor didn't give us much hope that it would ever happen. Paul and I began to pray and tell God that if He would give us a baby boy, we would give him back to Him.

Nothing happened immediately but a few months after the doctor gave us his opinion of our situation, I began to feel a little strange. Thinking I probably couldn't ever be pregnant, I thought I must be developing a tumor. When I went for a checkup, the doctor said, "I think this is the kind of tumor you've been wanting--you're pregnant."

Paul and I played it calm while we were in the doctor's

office but the minute we got outside his office door and closed it, we grabbed each other and danced up and down the hallway laughing. We were thrilled beyond words that we were going to have a baby!

Although the doctor said the baby had a tough time, this was an easy pregnancy and delivery for me.

He was such a good baby, such a blessing and a delight to raise. He was, and still is, a gift from God. We kept our end of the deal. We gave him back to God and God is using him to pastor, to write, to teach and to do public speaking whenever possible. He is used by God to enlighten and encourage countless others.

He truly is a gift from God to us, but God let me get to the place where instead of not wanting a "bunch" of children, I had to deal with perhaps not having any. I had to get to where I desired a child more than anything. This way I could appreciate the gift he was getting ready to give me. Thank you, Lord, for our wonderful baby boy.

"Every good thing bestowed and every perfect gift is from above, coming down from the Father of lights, with whom there is no variation, or shifting shadow."

(James 1:17)

THE LORD KNOWS WHAT WE NEED BEFORE WE ASK
by Alice

In 1960, Paul and I were expecting our second child. It had been difficult for me to get pregnant both times. To begin with, we had never been given much hope by the doctors that we would ever have any children. And yet, here I was pregnant again. Because of ovarian tumors, I had even had surgery a year or two earlier that had removed all my ovary tissue except for a small portion about the size of a fingernail, the doctor said.

Talk about miracles. In those days I didn't know to call them miracles, but that's what both pregnancies were. However, my time to deliver came and went with no sign of labor. I was getting bigger all the time. It was a hot summer and we had no air conditioning then, so the doctor decided to put me in the hospital even though it was only a short time after my calculated due date. He wanted to induce labor on me. They tried all their medicines for two days and nothing happened---not one contraction or even a hint of one. The third day the doctor decided to send me home to wait a while longer.

On that same day before I could leave, I started to turn over in my hospital bed and all of a sudden, my afterbirth gushed all over the bed. I should have been rushed immediately to surgery but they didn't do anything but wait for me to go into labor. I should have gone into hard labor, they said.

Our doctor was young, so he listened to the advice of two older, more hardened doctors, who thought they should wait. They did wait---until the next day. Finally, they took me to surgery and did a caesarean. Our baby was born dead. He weighed 9 lbs. and was 23 inches long and looked perfect and beautiful, Paul said. I was sure I had felt the baby move before I went to the operating room but the doctors told me I hadn't. They said I had only felt muscles contracting. I could have died, too, and it wouldn't have mattered to me at that time, except we had a beautiful little tow-headed four year old boy who still needed me.

After we had lost the baby people tried to console me with such things as, "He's in a better place," and "He won't have to live in this world." People even came to my hospital room and told me so many morbid tales that Paul had a "No Visitors" sign posted on my door.

Paul and little Paul David had a funeral for baby Timothy. I was still in the hospital. Paul was the most wonderful, thoughtful husband. He moved the baby bassinet out of our bedroom and got rid of all the baby clothes we had accumulated, bought a new mattress that we couldn't afford for our bed and changed the furniture around in our bedroom to make it easier for me to come home. It helped, tremendously.

However, that baby was a real person who lived and grew inside me for more than nine months. Although I never saw him, he was no less a being and we wanted him, planned for him and expected wonderful things of him. I nearly had a breakdown. If it hadn't been for caring for our other little boy and keeping my hands busy sewing, even sewing for other people, I would have been a basket case--actually, I was anyway, but I managed to keep my feelings inside. I made it through the days okay, but at nights when I went to bed and the house was quiet all I could do was think about Timothy and pray to God to take care of him. I prayed this prayer fervently as though God wouldn't take care of him unless I begged.

The three of us survived a year. We had lost something dear to us and there wasn't a thing we could do about it.

About a year after this happened, we read in our Baptist paper, *The Western Recorder*, that our Baptist adoption agency was taking applications from couples who desired a baby. Paul and I hardly had to discuss it. We wrote to the agency asking to adopt a baby. We had the regular paper work to fill out and then we were asked to come for an interview. A case worker also visited our home. The three of us went to Louisville and had a nice interview but little did we realize how closely they tried to match family backgrounds. We learned there were 24 other couples ahead of us on the adoptive parent's waiting list.

I was working for a dentist at the time. One day I answered his phone routinely and the voice on the other end said, "Is this Alice Prather? How would you like to have a baby girl?" We later learned that the agency had bypassed the other 24 couples after they met us in person. Not only did our backgrounds match that of the biological parents but we were told that the baby's biological mother and I would have passed for sisters.

The Lord knew what we had need of before we asked. The birth mother was already nearing her delivery time when we applied. I believe the Lord gave us a girl so we couldn't compare this baby with the baby boy we had lost. She was a beautiful, chubby, high-tempered baby who filled our home with what we had missed so much. We named her Cathi. She was sent to us to love and to fill the void we all had. Paul's mother said we were three of the saddest

13

people she had ever seen until the birth of Cathi and then we all came alive.

"The Lord knew what we had need of---before we asked."
(Based on Matthew 6:8)

WILL LIVES
by Paul

The final days of our daughter's pregnancy were difficult. She was in labor for several days. She would go to the doctor or the hospital and they would send her home. Finally, she was admitted to the hospital and after hours and hours of hard labor, her obstetrician decided to perform a caesarean. Alice and I had been waiting for days, so we were relieved when they finally decided to do something.

After what seemed to be an eternity, the nurse came and announced to us that we had a new grandson. We were on our way back to the recovery room to see our daughter and new grandson when we met the nurse running down the hall with him in her arms. She was headed for the neonatal unit with him. She just let us see him slightly. He looked so pale and lifeless.

The next time we saw him was in that unit. He had all sorts of wires and tubes hooked up to him. Our daughter asked us to pray for his recovery. We went home to call everyone we knew to pray. It was three o'clock in the afternoon when our people started praying. Some time later, our daughter called to tell us everything had changed and Will was going to be okay. We later found out he began to get better at the exact time we were praying for him ---3:00 p.m.

When the medical staff was asked what had been wrong with him, they said he had gotten well so quickly they didn't have time to diagnose his illness.

We learned God can heal so quickly that man cannot discover the problem.

Will, now 10, is a healthy boy active in school, sports and church.

"I, the Lord, am your healer . . ."
(Exodus 15:26)

WILL'S BIRTH
by Alice

Our daughter, Cathi, was pregnant with what was to be our second grandson. She had watched her diet the best she could. She even drank milk although she had never liked milk. She had smoked some up until she learned she was pregnant. She stopped that immediately. Her goal was to keep herself healthy and give her baby every chance to enter this world healthy, too.

Her marriage was a rocky one. She tried to be a good wife but sometimes the strain of everything was almost too much. As the time of the baby's arrival grew near, she realized that she was going to be mostly on her own. We were there to help however we could but we couldn't be a loving husband to her.

A week from delivery she began to have contractions, so we took her to the hospital. Nothing happened and we were sent home to wait. Waiting turned out to be light labor for six days. Then, the real thing came and we hurried her back to the hospital. She went into what seemed to be normal labor. It gradually progressed into hard labor that went on for hours. She could hardly bear it and we were helpless to do anything for her.

Cathi wanted so desperately to have this baby naturally but it just wasn't going to happen. The labor progressed to the danger stage--a little longer and Cathi and the baby were going to be in serious trouble. She finally agreed to have a caesarean section. We were relieved that it would soon be over.

Paul and I and our son and his family waited until the operation was over. We were told it was a boy. We were so happy. Paul and I were walking down a corridor to a door leading to the area where Cathi was when we met a nurse carrying a baby. He seemed to look at us with a soft, weak expression in his little eyes. We were so glad to see a real baby after all these days of waiting. But the nurse only paused for a spilt second to let us look at him. Then, she almost ran to the elevator to take him to the neonatal unit upstairs. He weighed 9 lbs. 6 ozs.---what in the world could be wrong with him?

He was hooked up to tubes and wires with one wire even stuck in his little head. He was such a big healthy looking baby in the unit compared to the premature babies who only weighed one and a half or two pounds. Something was wrong, though, and he needed help. We began to call people we knew and ask them to pray. We called on churches to pray and Paul called the 700 club and requested prayer. Our grandson began to get well immediately.

The doctors kept him in the neonatal unit for six days so he could be monitored. They were never able to find what was wrong with him because he recovered so fast.

Praise the Lord for the miracle we witnessed in our little grandson.

". . . 'Who are these with you?' So he said, 'The children whom God has graciously given your servant.'"
(Genesis 33:5)

HE SHALL BE CALLED JOHN
by Alice

John is our first grandson. He is twelve years old. Our son, Paul, and his wife, Renee, found out she was pregnant just as they were making a move to Lexington, Kentucky, to be closer to the University where Paul was a student.

The few months they lived in Lexington were very unpleasant. Renee was sick so much of the time. She would work at her job and they would go get a bite to eat. When they got home, she would have to go to bed. Neither of them had any experience with a baby and when John was born, they hardly knew what to do with him. They had been married for a few years before his birth and they were used to sleeping when they felt like it and watching a movie when they felt like it. Now, here was this baby who screamed a lot and slept very little. I remember them telling about one incident when they had done everything they could for John and he still screamed. They stood helplessly in the kitchen and just looked at each other and said, "What in the world are we doing with a baby?" However, they soon caught on and became wonderful parents.

The night the baby was born, a waiting room full of family members sat the night out talking and wondering what was going on in there, little did we know that Renee was having such a terrible time. Paul couldn't leave her side to come out and give us a progress report.

She had gone to the hospital armed with all the equipment the Lamaze instructors had taught her to use--a rubber ball to squeeze when the contractions came, thick wool socks to keep her feet warm, and numerous other items. All these could have helped in a normal delivery but John's arrival was not normal. Little did we know that John had been born compound: his leg entered the birth canal the same time his head did. This was not only excruciating for Renee, but it nearly dislocated John's hip. Paul had to watch as the doctor placed the baby on the table and moved a little flopping leg around. The leg looked like it was broken but as the doctor worked with it, it began to go in place and was fine.

He was fine all over and at last we were told we could go to the nursery window where we would be able to see him. We rushed to the window where we oohed and aahed and made all the silly faces people make at a new baby.

We watched as the nurse worked with the baby while he desperately tried to sleep. He had been through an ordeal and he was exhausted. As she moved him around, he frowned and cried to the top of his lungs. When she left him alone, he immediately settled down into a deep sleep again.

We laughed at what we were witnessing but we were so thankful for what the Lord had done. John could easily have been born with a broken leg but he was healthy. Renee had suffered so much and yet, her recovery was a fast one.

We had just witnessed the wonderful miracle of birth!

". . .he shall be called John."
(Luke 1:60)

MY BIRTH IS AN ACT OF GOD
by Paul

My mother had given birth to a son and three daughters before I was born. She loved them dearly but was not satisfied because she wanted another son. She prayed for years after the youngest daughter was born, "Father, give me another son." Sometime within the six years before I was conceived, she added, "And I will give him back to you." The Lord heard her prayer and she conceived again in early 1930. From what she told me, I learned it was not an easy pregnancy.

Sometime in the seventh month, she was helping hang wallpaper in their house when she fell off the stepladder. She took a terrible blow and began to bleed profusely. Dad took her to their doctor who examined her, sent her back home, and told her to go to bed and stay there until the baby was born. So, for the better part of two months she remained in bed. Finally, on October 4, 1930, I came into this world. God had "heard and answered my prayer," she often said. "You are my miracle baby," she would tell me as she hugged me up close and read the Bible to me. Many times she said, "You are going to be something special because God gave you to me and I have given you back to him."

All my life she encouraged me to be the best I could be. She expected me to be the head of my class, to go to college, and to do what was right.

Because of her faith in me, I was the first in my family

to attend college. She was so proud of me when I graduated.

One time when I was about 10 or 11 years old, I got really smart-mouthed with an older woman because she threatened to kill my dog for chasing her chickens. By the time I got home I was furious. I told mother what had happened and that I had said, "If you kill my dog, I'll kill every one of your old chickens!" Guess what mother did! She marched me right back up to see that woman. She even made me go in by myself to tell her I was sorry I had talked to her like I did and ask her to forgive me. The woman forgave me and followed me back home crying, asking for forgiveness for herself.

I was very fortunate to get started in life by a God fearing mother who believed God for a son whom she could give back to Him.

"Delight thyself in the Lord and He will give you the desires of thy heart."

(Psalm 37:4)

MOTHER'S EYE HEALED
by Paul

In the early 1970s my mother was stricken with cancer, which eventually took her life. She was in the Somerset, Kentucky, City Hospital. We lived in Campbellsville, Kentucky, where I was on the staff of the Baptist college.

One day when I made the 50-mile trip to Somerset to see her, I found her with a patch over her left eye. When she took the patch loose so that I could see her eye, I saw the proud flesh coming out. She could not see out of this eye.

Before I left that day, she said to me, "Son, the only thing I have ever really asked the Lord for myself is not go blind. Please pray for me that I won't lose my sight." I had never seen God heal anyone, didn't really know about instant healings, and was skeptical of the results. I took her hands in mine and mustered up as much faith and courage as I possibly could and prayed for the Lord to heal her eye. Soon after praying, I left for home wondering what the results might be.

A few days later I went back to see her. I was amazed! The patch was gone from her eye and she could see better out of it than she could her "good eye." She must have had enough faith for both of us because her eye wasn't healed because of my faith--I didn't have any. One of her doctors told me, "It's a miracle. We didn't do anything that might heal that eye."

After this incident she became unable to walk and had to be taken to a convalescent center in a neighboring town.

She was very dissatisfied there. When we would go to visit her, she would say, "I am going to walk out of here and go home to Somerset (Kentucky)." There was a milk delivery truck from Somerset which came to the center regularly. She would tell us that one day she was going to walk out, get on that truck, and go home. At this time, she could not walk a step but she had faith and was determined that she would walk again. She couldn't write either, but she kept trying.

She remained in the convalescent center for several months. One day after an absence of several days, I went back to see her. She said, "Look, son, at what I can do!" With much effort, she pulled herself up out of her wheelchair and started to take a few steps. I began to yell, "Mother, be careful!" She walked across the room and back to her chair.

Then, she began to write. She wrote and wrote and kept all of her writings on a paper tablet. She began to write her memoirs with the hope they would one day be published.

When I went to see her at the center one day, she said to me, "Son, of all the people in the world, I didn't think you would ever leave me in a place like this." My heart broke right in two pieces. I left there that day thinking, "Mother, as soon as I can do something about this, I will get you out of here." I went home and told Alice that I didn't know what it would lead to but I was taking her out of that rest home and bringing her to our house. My family warned me against doing this but Alice and I determined it was the only thing left for us to do. So, I went to the center, checked her out, and brought her to our home. She stayed with us for several months and continued to get stronger. She finished her memoirs there.

One of my sisters who lived in California decided to

come back to Kentucky, to take her home to Somerset, and stay with her until we could find someone else to stay.

I took mother and my sister to mother's home in Somerset. When we went in the front door, she began to shout, "I'm home! I'm home! Praise the Lord! I'm home!" My sister and brother found a woman to stay with her so that she could spend her last days at home. We went to visit her as often as possible and took her shopping when she felt up to it. After my sister went back to California, my brother continued to care for her and dad until they died. Mother died in her own bed at home at the age of 76.

I learned many valuable lessons during this period. One of them was: When we trust in the Lord, He can make a way when there is no way!

"Delight yourself in the Lord; and He will give you the desires of your heart."

(Psalm 37:4)

EYES AND EARS OPENED
by Paul

Two of the most remarkable things I have seen God do are to open blind eyes and deaf ears. I have already written about my mother's eye being healed of cancer. I want to tell more about witnessing blind eyes see and deaf ears hear.

One of my first times to speak at a Full Gospel Business Men's Fellowship International chapter meetings was in Columbia, Kentucky. After I had spoken, people came forward to be prayed for. One woman said she was deaf in her right ear. She asked me to pray that her ear would be healed. I put my finger in the opening of her right ear and asked God to heal her. Then, I took my hand away from her and whispered to someone near me. When I did, she evidently realized that God had touched her because she heard my whispers. She began to yell very loudly, "I can hear! I can hear! Praise the Lord, I can hear!" We did several other impromptu tests to see if she was really healed. She passed every test.

I spoke in a meeting in a church in Charlestown, Indiana, for a week. In one of these services, a woman with a blind eye came forward for prayer. When I prayed for her, she fell in the floor under the power of God. She lay in the floor for quite some time.

When she came to herself, she quickly got up off of the floor, covered her good eye with her hand and began to shout, "My eye is healed! I can see! I can see better out of this eye than I can out of the other one!" We continued to test her eye and concluded she had been healed, her sight had been restored.

Jesus said, "The works that I do shall you do and greater works than these shall you do." He opened deaf ears and blind eyes and gave us the authority to do the same.

I learned from this experience, and others, that we have far more power than we have ever realized. If we really believe, signs and wonders will be following us.

Jesus said,
"These signs shall follow those who believe . . ."
(Mark 16:17)

THE LAME WALK
by Paul

I was the speaker at a Full Gospel Business Men's chapter meeting in Jackson, Tennessee.

Before it was time for me to speak, I looked toward the back of the room and saw some people bringing a woman into the meeting in a wheelchair. In my spirit, I heard the Lord say, "I am going to heal that woman tonight." It really startled me because I had never seen anyone in a wheelchair healed.

As I approached the speaker's stand, I saw the woman seated on the front row to the left in her wheelchair. I could hardly give my testimony knowing that I was going to have to pray for her and get her up out of that chair. Finally, after I had given my testimony and prayed for everyone else who came forward, I went over to her and asked her some questions. First, I asked her how long it had been since she had walked. "Ten years," she told me. It had been five years since she had stood alone. Then, I asked her what she wanted to receive from the Lord. "I want to walk," she said. Hoping she would answer the next question more vaguely, I asked, "When do you want to walk?" Without hesitation she replied, "Now!"

I had never quite been on this spot before. I had to produce. This was real. No fun and games at this point. I silently prayed, "Lord, give me strength. Give me faith. Give me power." I was trembling as I reached out my hand to her and said the only thing I knew to say, "In the name of

Jesus, get up and walk!" I helped her with one hand. Praise the Lord! She stood by herself for the first time in five years.

Turning her hand loose and backing away from her, I said, "Now walk to me." She took a couple of feeble steps and walked to me. I backed away from her some more and she walked to me. We kept repeating this procedure until she had walked across the room by herself. She then turned and walked back to her chair unassisted. God had heard her prayer. She had walked, "Now."

*"Go and report to John what you have seen and heard: the blind receive sight, **the lame walk**, the lepers are cleansed, and the deaf hear . . . "*

(Luke 7:22)

BROKEN BONES HEALED
by Paul

When our daughter was still in high school, she worked briefly at the local McDonalds restaurant.

One evening she went outside for something, slipped, fell, and broke her arm. The manager wanted to take her to the hospital but she insisted on going home first. By the time she arrived home the arm had swollen, was beginning to change color, and the bone was almost protruding through the skin. I have seen a lot of broken bones. This one definitely was broken. I told her I thought we should take her to the hospital. She didn't want to go. "Lay hands on it and pray for it and I believe God will heal it," she said. I said I did not have enough faith to believe for a broken bone.

But, our son was present, too, and he said, "I do. Let me pray for it." The family gathered around her to pray. He prayed a real prayer of faith. I had her hand in mine while he prayed and I felt the arm move back into place. When we looked at the arm, the bone was no longer protruding. The severe pain had diminished. It was obvious to us that God had touched and healed her arm. Some swelling and discoloration remained for a few days but she didn't have to go to the hospital, nor even see a doctor.

God taught us a valuable lesson -- He heals broken bones when someone has enough faith to pray and believe.

"Many are the afflictions of the righteous; but the Lord delivers them out of them all. He keeps all his bones; not one of them is broken."

(Psalm 34:19-20)

I HATE TO GO TO THE DENTIST
by Alice

I'm not one to keep regular appointments at the dentist's office. In fact, I put my visits off for years sometimes. For one thing, I'm a procrastinator. For another thing, going to the dentist is just not my favorite thing to do. Dumb? Very! But I may as well be honest. These are words coming from a former dental assistant. I've looked in lots of people's mouths and I know a little bit about teeth. Another thing is, we've never had dental insurance or big bucks to spend on such things, so it's been easy to put off my visits.

Year before last, I discovered a cavity in one of my few remaining teeth, a front tooth at that. Instead of rushing to the dentist as most intelligent people would, you guessed it, I waited. After several months of trying not to think about it, I saw my dentist in a restaurant downtown and said to him, "I'm going to have to come and see you." "I'm still in the same place," he said. I guess he realized it had been a long time since he had seen me.

I still waited. I guess I'm just plain chicken. One morning as I was dressing, I decided I would take a peek at my cavity. I had to go to the dentist. As I pulled down my lip to look at the ugly sight, it was gone! The cavity had disappeared. The tooth didn't show any signs of a cavity or of there ever having been one. The Lord had healed it. There was no other explanation. I was planning on going to the dentist to get it filled.

The thing that really got my attention was this--I hadn't

even asked the Lord to heal it. I wasn't expecting a miracle. I was expecting a trip to the dentist. This was such a humbling experience for me. In my spirit I felt the Lord saying, "See, I care for you in ways you aren't even asking me for. I'm looking out for your welfare--you have no need to worry about anything."

I didn't deserve this. I wasn't filled with faith to get the tooth filled. God did it because He wanted to, I think, to show me He knows where I am and what I need.

God knows where you are, too. Don't ever think for a moment He has forgotten you.

"Casting all your anxiety upon Him, because He cares for you."

(I Peter 5:7)

I NEVER SAW THE LIKE
by Alice

The first time I ever saw a tooth that had been filled by God was when Paul was in the hospital after having been diagnosed with terminal cancer. There was another patient across the hall, a Baptist like us, with cancer, too. We and his wife, Rose, spent quite a bit of time talking about things as they seemed to be and as we hoped they would be. One day Rose told this story.

She said she had been needing to have some dental work done but there was no way they could afford it because their medical bills had been astronomical since her husband had been ill. One night she was awake as her husband slept, worrying about the large cavity in her tooth and feeling so helpless to have anything done about it. Suddenly, she began to taste novocaine in her mouth. She eased out of the bed, slipped into the bathroom, and shut the door so she wouldn't awaken her husband when she turned on the light. She stood in front of the mirror and opened her mouth. To her surprise, she saw that her tooth had been filled.

This story absolutely beat anything I had ever heard. I had formerly worked as a dental assistant. Consequently, I had looked into lots of mouths and had seen lots of fillings. So I said to Rose, "Come over by the window and let me look in your mouth." She did, and I had never seen, and still haven't seen, a filling to compare with hers. The filling was in a molar. It was bronze with ever-so-tiny gold flecks (this probably gave it the bronze look).

The dentist will usually finish his work with an instrument that enables him to make little designs in the tooth that resemble the shape of a normal tooth. Rose's filling had a smooth look. I'm sure my surprise--no, shock--showed in my face. Never had I seen anything that looked like this.

Little did I know the Lord was working on me, that He was getting ready to show me miracles of His watch care, His love. He was starting to teach me things I never dreamed were possible. He's still teaching me and I hope He never stops.

Rose, if you read this---thank you for sharing this blessing with us and God bless you! Come to think of it, God bless you even if you don't read this!

"It is good to give thanks to the Lord . . ."
(Psalm 92:1)

GOD LOVES DOGS
by Paul

We have always loved dachshunds and have owned several of them. When we got involved in the Charismatic movement, we had one named "Bismarck." These dogs often are bothered with back trouble. Bismarck often whined and cried because his back was hurting. His favorite place to lie down when he was suffering was on the floor in front of the refrigerator where the warm air from the motor came out.

One day Bismarck was lying in this spot. He was really in bad shape. When he tried to walk, he dragged his hind feet across the floor. My son and I had just finished having a prayer time together. We were really keyed up. We wanted to find someone to lay hands on and pray for but there was no one around. One of us said to the other, "Do you suppose God would heal a dog's back if we prayed for him?" "I don't see why not," the other said.

Simultaneously we laid our hands on that dog and said, "In the name of Jesus, be healed!" The dog twisted his back, yelped loudly, and got up off of the floor healed -- running at full speed.

Bismarck never had back trouble again and lived to a ripe old age. The Lord taught me that He cares for animals, too.

"For whoever is joined with all the living, there is hope; surely a live dog is better than a dead lion."

(Ecclesiastes 9:4)

SECTION 2

FINANCIAL MIRACLES

$1000
by Paul

On one occasion I desperately needed $1000 to pay income taxes. I went to the church study to pray. There, I fell down on my knees, and then on my face before the Lord. I cried out to Him, "Lord, you know I need this money today." Tears flowed like a river. Suddenly, it was as if someone took me by the shirt collar, pulled me up from the floor, and stood me on my feet. In my spirit, I heard the voice of the Lord say, "Get out of here and do something for someone, who can't do anything for you. Quit whimpering and crying and trust me."

I washed my face, tried to look happy, and started out to visit an invalid woman whom I knew who had no worldly goods to share with me. I often went to see her just to pray for her and try to be a friend in the time of her loneliness. When I got to her apartment and went in she said, "You have a financial need, don't you?" I told her she was right and asked her how she knew. She said that the Lord had come by to visit her and told her about it "night before last." Then, she said "He not only told me about your need, He brought the money to take care of it."

Knowing she had no earthly goods and that she lived in government housing, subsisting on welfare and a little Social Security, I was skeptical. I thought, "Yeah, you probably could give me $5, or maybe even $25, but I need $1000"

She gave me a long speech on God's watch care and the

many ways that He could take of us. After what seemed to be an eternity, she told me to get her Bible from a table across the room and open it to the very back. "The Lord came by here night before last and left you the money to pay what you need," she said. Still with some skepticism, I opened the Bible and looked where she had directed me. There, to my amazement, was a fresh bundle of one hundred dollar bills--ten of them : $1000!

I excitedly yelled, "Miss Bess, where did you get this money?" "I told you," she replied, "the Lord came by here night before last and left it for you!" I insisted that I could not take this money---she needed it worse than I did. "You have to take it," she said, "The Lord left it for you." No amount of protesting could change her mind. She vowed that the Lord had come by and left that money for me. She convinced me that none of it was her money. Therefore, I took the money.

One valuable lesson I learned from this was: The Lord knows what you have need of before you ask (Matt. 6:8)!

I also learned that if we trust God, He will care for us in His own way.

By the way, this wonderful lady went home to be with the Lord, still sticking to her statement: "The Lord came by and left you this money."

"And do not seek what you shall eat, and what you shall drink, and do not keep worrying . . . But seek for His kingdom and all these things shall be added unto you."
(Luke 12:29,31)

HE PROVIDES
by Paul

I was hospitalized in January, February, and part of March in 1976. Cancer was diagnosed and I was given from two to six months to live. (This story is told in another chapter). Through this experience the Lord taught me something about His providential care.

Before I was hospitalized, I had begun to study about God's care for His children. I was learning from the writings of great men and women of God such as Kenneth Hagin, Oral Roberts, Kenneth Copeland, Kathryn Kulhman and others, as well as from the Bible, that God is the only one we need to tell our needs to.

One of the stories I read was about a man who felt led of God to pledge several thousand dollars to a ministry. The only trouble was that he didn't have the money. He decided to go to the bank and borrow the money. After getting the money, he went out on the street to go home and met a woman he knew. The woman handed him an envelope with the exact amount of money he had borrowed in it. This and other such stories convinced me that God will provide for all our needs by whatever means it takes, even if He has to fly a helicopter over and drop the money out.

We had hospitalization insurance to take care of our hospital bill and 80 percent of our doctor bills. Many other expenses such as gasoline, food, incidental items, and personal needs were not covered. It was an expensive experience and we did not have enough money to take care of them. However, I told the Father what we needed and He saw that all our needs were met.

One day we went to the mail box and there was an envelope with $100 in it. Another day a neighbor came to our house and gave me $300. Cards came with money in them. Visitors gave us money. Money, prayers, and good wishes came our way constantly during my stay in the hospital. God had moved on the hearts of people to take care of all our needs. When I checked out, we only owed about $18 and we had the money to pay that.

I learned a vital lesson during this experience: If we really have faith, we only need to tell our Father what our needs are and he will take care of them! Paul put it this way:

"My God shall supply all your needs according to his riches in glory through Christ Jesus."

(Philippians 4:19)

$285 AT PRINCETON
by Paul

God often goes to great lengths to care for us, and to answer our prayers.

A few years ago I had a need for $285. At the time I had a small antiques business. One day about 10:00 a.m., I said to the Lord, "You know I need $285 today."

In about an hour a car pulled up in our parking lot. When the couple got out of the car and entered the store, I found out they were from Seattle, Washington. The husband was attending a convention in Atlanta, Georgia. They had rented a car in Atlanta and driven north through South and North Carolina, Virginia, West Virginia, and into Kentucky. They were traveling west through Kentucky on Interstate 65 which brought them to the outskirts of Mt. Sterling, Kentucky. When they got near Mt. Sterling, they decided to get off the interstate and travel U.S. 60 which brought them past our antiques shop.

The couple began to pick out little items which they could pack in their luggage and take back with them on their flight home. After choosing several small items, the husband asked, "If we buy some larger items, can you ship them to us." I told him I could, and they picked out an old kitchen cabinet (which I considered junk) to be shipped to them. Also, they picked out a few other items. We figured up what they owed me, not counting tax and shipping. You have probably already figured it out, my profit on what they bought came to exactly $285. They also left their credit card number to pay for shipping and crating.

The Lord taught me again that He knew what we had need of before we asked. They started from Seattle days before that prayer was lifted up, drove from Atlanta, though three other states to get to Mt. Sterling to answer my prayer at the very right time.

He also taught me that He will go to any lengths to do what His children ask.

"If you abide in me, and my words abide in you, ask whatever you wish, and it shall be done for you."

(John 15:7)

HELP FROM COLORADO SPRINGS
by Paul

Since a large part of my ministry has consisted of being pastor of small churches with low budgets, we have always had to depend on income from sources outside the local church to meet our expenses. Once, we had two different people who were supporting us with regular offerings. Each of them told me within the same month that God was leading them to give their offerings somewhere else.

This was a devastating blow to our finances. However, I began to remind God of His promises because He said, "Call me to remembrance." (Isaiah 43:26). I said to Him, "Father, You said in your Word . . . ," and, "I believe Your Word." Confessing His Word and believing in your heart bring results from Him.

Shortly after I got this troubling news from my two supporters, I received a phone call on a Sunday morning from a young woman who had attended a Bible study which I had taught in another city some years before. She asked about the time of our church services and informed me she would be in the services that morning. I learned she had moved to Colorado Springs, Colorado. She was visiting part of her family who lived in a nearby city and friends who lived in the general area of our church. Some of them wanted her to attend our services with them.

After the services were over, as she was leaving the church building, she very unassumingly shook hands with me. In her hand was a check which she had brought with her from Colorado. She explained she had been praying about where to give this money, and God had impressed on her to give it to me personally.

I put the check in my pocket to look at later. When I got alone where I was able to look at the check privately, I was elated to see the amount was for several hundred dollars---more than enough to pay my remaining bills for the month. I realized again that God knew what we needed before we asked. He knew in Colorado and brought it to me in Kentucky.

"Let us hold fast the confession of our faith without wavering, for He who promised is faithful . . ."

(Hebrews 10:23)

GET OUT OF BUSINESS
by Paul

About two years ago, I got into a business which had the potential of making a lot of money. A very good friend of mine, his wife, and son were all in the business. The son had become a millionaire in it. I was invited to a meeting to explore the possibility of becoming a representative. When I heard the son, who was named Paul after me, make his presentation, I said, "If Paul can do this, I can do it, too."

Almost immediately I signed up, persuaded that I could do the selling. This was in April. It was obvious to me that by the first of the year I could be making $10,000 a month like many other representatives were doing. I set out to become wealthy. I worked hard, which resulted in a quick, modest success. It looked like I was on my way to great fortunes.

Alice and I took a trip in November to London, Kentucky, to hear Charles Capps, a popular minister who majors on positive speaking. During the first meeting, I was trying my best to follow Capps' teaching but I had this overwhelming awareness of the presence of God and felt He was trying to speak to me. I quit trying to follow Capps and said in my spirit, "Speak, Lord, for thy servant is listening!" He did speak and I heard Him loudly and clearly.

What I heard Him say to me was, "You have left your first love and are trying to make it on your own." I sat there with my eyes closed, listening to the Lord. "I will take care of your needs, Myself," the Lord said.

Alice thought I had fallen asleep. She punched me and said, "Wake up!" However, I was not asleep. The Lord was speaking to me in my spirit and I wanted to hear what He was saying.

As you can imagine, when I told Alice what I felt like the Lord had spoken to me she said, "Are you sure?" I was sure. I made up my mind right then to do what God had told me to do. I decided to give up the businesses I had and trust in Him to care for all our needs.

The next day, soon after we had arrived home, a man who was just a casual acquaintance drove into our driveway, got out of his car, and gave me an offering--two $100 bills. "I was praying today and God told me to give you this offering," he said. The next day he gave me another $100, saying, "I didn't do all God told me to do." Then, the next day he gave me another $200, then the next day another $100. He kept this up until he had given me $1000.

I felt God speak to me in my spirit again. He seemed to say, "See, if I had this man waiting to meet your needs at this time, don't you see that I can meet any other needs you have?"

Up to this very day, God has met all my needs through His riches in Christ Jesus!

" I pray that the eyes of your heart may be enlightened, so that you may know what is . . . the riches of the glory of His inheritance in the saints, and what is the surpassing greatness of His power toward us who believe."

(Ephesians 1:18-19)

$235 AT PRINCETON
by Paul

I used to teach a Bible study group in Princeton, Kentucky. It was a five-hour drive from Mt. Sterling and, consequently, expensive since I had to stay overnight in a motel and pay my own lodging and travel costs. Each time we met, the group took a love offering to help me. The offerings usually ran around $100. This was adequate, since it usually cost me about $80 or $90 to make the trip.

On one certain meeting day, I was particularly low on finances. In fact, I did not have enough to meet the costs of the trip. I was going "on faith." On the way there, I began to pray about the offering because I not only needed the money to pay for the trip but I also needed to meet some bills when I got back home.

I was impressed to pray for a certain amount --$235, as I recall. This was much more than I had ever received at this meeting. When I arrived at the meeting place, the crowd was extremely small and my faith began to waver slightly. When the offering was handed to me at the close of the service, it was exactly the amount for which I had asked.

The Lord taught me a valuable lesson: Don't look at the size of the crowd because He fed five thousand with five barley loaves and two fish. For me, the old adage "don't count your chickens before they hatch" became "don't count your offering before you receive it."

". . .we look not at the things which are seen, but at the things which are not seen . . ."

(II Corinthians 4:18)

HE PROVIDES CLOTHES
by Paul

I have learned that our Father is concerned about our clothing needs.

A few years ago, I needed a new suit. At the same time, a local department store was having a sale on men's clothing. I went to look at their suits. They had one I particularly liked. It was priced at $110 plus tax, making a total of $116. All I could afford was the $16, which I paid as a down payment to put it on lay away. I asked God to provide the rest of the money to pay for it. That was on a Saturday.

The next day when we got to church, as I was walking across the lawn from one building to another, one of the men of the church yelled for me to wait up. When he came over to where I was, he handed me a check for $100. "I was praying last night and I felt like the Lord told me to give you this to buy you a new suit," he said. He had no way of knowing anything about what had taken place the day before. I told the people in church that day about this. The next day when I went to get the suit, someone else had already been in the store and paid for it!

On another occasion I found a suit I needed in the same store. It had been $160 but was now on sale, in my size, for $40. It had been through several sales because it had the wrong size on the tag. It was the only one in the store in my size in that price range. I felt as if it had been kept in the store just for me but I didn't have any money, except for a small amount which was needed for another bill. I decided to go to my wife's office and see what she thought about me using that money to pay for the suit.

On the way to see her I decided to stop and return a book to a friend. I intended to simply stop, hand the book in the door, and be on my way. I stopped, stood in the doorway, and returned the book. As I was standing there talking to my friend his wife yelled, "If that's Brother Prather, tell him to come in, I want to see him!"

When I stepped into the room, she motioned for me to sit down on the couch by her. She had brought her purse with her. While she was opening her purse and digging through it, she said, "The Lord told me this morning to give you a love offering. It's not much but it is what He told me to do." She handed me two $20 bills, exactly what I needed for the suit. I went back to the store, paid for the suit, and took it to my wife's office to show her what the Lord had done.

Once, I had needed a new pair of dress shoes. I asked the Lord for a new pair of wingtips. On a Sunday after church, one of the young single women who attended our services said to me, "Here is an offering. Don't be mad at me but the Lord told me to buy you a new pair of shoes!" When I opened the envelope she had given me, there was exactly enough money to buy a new pair of wingtips.

"Take no thought about what we eat, or what we drink, or what we wear. The Father knows we have need of these things."

(Matt.6: 31-33)

NEW CLOTHES
by Alice

What woman doesn't care about clothes? Oh, we may not all be known as clotheshorses, but there probably isn't a woman reading this book who doesn't know what a new dress or a new pair of shoes or even new underwear can do for our self-confidence. Especially when we can look in the mirror and feel good about what we see!

Jesus said we shouldn't take any thought about what we wear (or eat or drink) for our heavenly Father who takes care of the sparrows and the lilies will take care of our needs. Now, either Jesus wasn't speaking this to the women or it had another meaning. I suspect it means that we aren't to gripe and complain about what we have or don't have to wear--whichever the case might be. If there is a lack, we should simply tell our heavenly Father and then leave it there.

As a working, churchgoing woman, I need several outfits. They don't have to be expensive, designer clothes but they need to be the right color for me, comfortable, something I can afford and something I feel good in.

A few years ago I learned a valuable lesson I want to pass on to you because the principle works whether you are male or female and it doesn't just have to do with clothes. Think what your need is . . .

I went to the closet to get something out to wear and my choice was slim to little. But I still remember my thoughts and feelings as though it were last week. I simply said,

"Father, I need some new clothes."

I took down an outfit and put it on and went my way. Within a week or two I came across a good sale and every woman loves a good sale! I was able to buy two or three outfits very reasonably. When I took them home and hung them in the closet, it was as though a light came on in my spirit and I realized my prayer had been answered. I didn't have to do any whining, begging, or worrying about when and how I was going to get something to wear. I had just told my heavenly Father my need and left it at that.

Do you have a need? Tell the One who cares, but don't be anxious.

"For this reason I say to you, do not be anxious for your life, as to what you shall eat; nor for your body, as to what you shall put on."

(Luke 12:22)

NEW BEDROOM SUITE
by Paul

A few years before Alice and I moved to Mt. Sterling, Kentucky, we bought our only bedroom suite and gave $80 for it. It was previously owned but it was very nice. We used it for several years --- and then gave it to our son and his wife when they got married. We used a metal portable fame with box springs and mattress to make us a temporary king-sized bed. We used it for several years alongside used chests and dressers.

I had also bought a vintage car for myself--a 1956 Edsel. During a week of revival at our church, I felt led to give the Edsel to the missionary-evangelist who was conducting our revival. I figured the car to be worth about $1000 at the time. At least, the evangelist sold it the next day for $1000, and I was happy to see him get that much.

A few days later, I stopped by a furniture store in Lexington to see a friend who owned the store. "Bring your wife by the store one day soon," he said. "The Lord has told me and my wife to give you a new bedroom suite." I was so astounded that I rushed out of the store, breaking the speed limit to get home. All the way home I kept saying, "Lord, you beat all!"

A short time later we drove back to the store to look around. We were looking for the cheapest thing we could find when the owner walked up and said, "You don't want any of this furniture, it's my cheaper line. You deserve the best!" Leading the way, he took us to the room where the expensive furniture was displayed. "Could you use a king sized outfit?" he asked. Assuring him we could, we were shocked when he gave us a bedroom suite worth more than $6000 retail. It was solid cherry with a beautiful poster bed, a triple dresser, a highboy, two night tables, and an armoire. He even gave us expensive box springs and a mattress which added to the price.

Alice and I have had a good-natured discussion down through the years about why the Lord did this for us. She says it is because we gave away our bedroom suite. I say it is because I gave my Edsel for missions.

Either way, we couldn't out give God!

"Give and it shall be given unto you . . ."
(Luke 6:38)

REFRIGERATORS
by Paul

I have learned that God is concerned about refrigerators. We had one refrigerator which lasted for a number of years. Then, it began to die. One day it finally 'gave up the ghost.' Alice decided to practice what we had been believing---God answers prayer. She laid hands on that refrigerator and commanded it to work in the Name of Jesus. It ran and did well for a several more years.

We did not know that a refrigerator should not be laid on its side when it was being moved. Our son, Paul, and I moved the refrigerator and laid it on its side. Well, that was the end of that refrigerator. "When we get a new one, I want a side-by-side," Alice said. A side-by-side refrigerator is one with a freezer on one side and the refrigerator on the other.

One of the men of our church who was helping us with some plumbing work said that he had a used refrigerator we could have. His little boy had flipped the off switch and they did not find it out until they had already bought a new one. Guess what? When we went to get that refrigerator, it was a side-by-side! We used that refrigerator for about seven or eight years and it started to go bad. The repairman told us to shoot it and have its funeral. We began to look for a new one.

In the meantime, I preached in a church in Lexington, Kentucky, on a Thursday night and received a nice love offering but it was not nearly enough to buy a new refrigerator. We found one like Alice wanted for $649. We started to figure out how to get enough money to buy it.

On Monday or Tuesday of the next week an anonymous letter came with a note in it from someone who had been in the church service on the previous Thursday night. The person explained that he (or she) was in the service and God had moved on him (or her) to send me a check as a love offering. It was for $640. When we told the merchant we were going to pay cash, he took off $10.

We learned again that God cares about all our needs, and He will provide for us if we trust Him.

"Trust in the Lord with all your heart, and do not lean to your own understanding. In all your ways acknowledge Him, and He shall direct your paths . . ."

(Proverbs 3:5-6)

GOING TO CALIFORNIA
by Paul

In 1977 my sister, Hazel, who lived in California was afflicted with cancer. She asked me to fly out there just to pray for her. I went at her expense. We had a great time talking, praying, and renewing our relationship. When I prayed for her I felt she was really touched by the Lord, but for some unknown reason she died ten days later. I was called to return for her funeral. I didn't really want to go because I did not have the money and, besides, I had just gotten back from a trip to pray for her and I felt like a failure.

I felt like the Lord spoke to me and told me He wanted me to go. I felt like His message to me was that I had not failed. On the contrary, I had done all I could do. I had done my part; the rest was in His hands. I said, "But, Lord, I don't have the money." I felt again that He spoke to me in my spirit and said, "You make the airline reservations and I will provide the money." So, I called Delta and made reservations. The round trip ticket was $298.

Immediately after I got off the telephone, two different men called me asking me to come by their businesses that morning. One of them invited me to lunch. Each of them said (not knowing anything about what the other one had done), "I was praying this morning and God told me you had a financial need." Each one reached into his billfold and gave me a $100 bill! But, that was only $200 and I needed at least $300. Nothing else happened, no more money came in, but I knew what God had told me.

Late that afternoon, I went to see our Sunday school director to tell him I was leaving and would not be at church on Sunday. When I walked into his office, his boss said, "Where have you been? I've been looking for you for the most part of the day. This morning I was praying and the Lord told me you have a financial need. He told me to give you this $100 to help you." There it was---the rest of the money to make the trip.

This happened on a Wednesday. I went to the midweek service that night and told the congregation what had happened. One of the ladies in the service came up to me after the service was over, handed me a $20 bill and said, "Here, buy yourself something to eat." I made the trip and came home with $10 left.

God taught me that He can make a way when there is no way.

"Trust in the Lord, and do good . . .Delight yourself in the Lord; and He will give you the desires of your heart."

(Psalm 37:3-4)

"Trust in the Lord at all times . . ."

(Psalm 62:8)

A NEW CAR
by Paul

In 1978 I was driving a 1973 Oldsmobile to the meetings where I was speaking. It was in good condition, therefore, I expected to drive it to many other meetings for a number of years.

Our church was having a weekend meeting. A minister from Indiana, George Gray, was speaking for us. On Sunday afternoon, George and I were out visiting prospects when I received a telephone call telling me that our daughter had wrecked our car but neither she nor her passenger was hurt. Immediately, from deep within there came out words of praise, "Praise God, He is getting ready to do something better for us!"

I had the car towed to Queen Chevrolet-Oldsmobile. The next day I found out the car was a total loss. I did not have insurance on my own car. When I saw Mr. Queen, I began to talk to him about making arrangements to get another car. He said, "I believe God wants you to have a new car. Go out on the lot and pick out a car and we will see what we can do." I found a new 1978 Oldsmobile station wagon I liked very much. He told me I could have the car at his cost, and he would pay the tax and title. I considered this a generous offer but I did not have the income to make a car payment.

I told one of the men of my church about this and he said, "I don't see why the men of the church can't buy this for you." He said he would pay the first payment and help with the other payments. He told the other men of the church about this and they agreed among themselves to put enough extra money in the offering each month to make the payments, which they did.

So, what the devil intended for evil the Lord turned around for my good. On Tuesday I was driving a new Oldsmobile station wagon and it did not cost me anything -- not one penny.

Before we drove the car out of the garage, my son and I laid hands on it and openly prayed a prayer of dedication, giving this car to the Lord. I drove it for 92,000 miles without changing the plugs. I was involved in an accident when the car had 198,000 miles on the speedometer. It had never had a serious repair job and was running like new when it was destroyed in the wreck. Once again, God had provided for my need in a very special way.

"My God shall supply all your needs according to his riches in glory through Christ Jesus."

(Philippians 4:19)

A CALL FROM FLORIDA
by Paul

From what I have written in these stories, it would seem I am always in need of money. That is not the case at all. I feel God has kept me on the edge many times so I can learn to trust Him. Maybe He has kept me here so I can write these stories down because those who need a boost in their faith can read them and be lifted up.

Once when I needed some money, I received a call from a friend in Florida who had gone there for a few days. He said, "This morning as I was praying I got these strong feelings that you needed some money. As I prayed, the sum of $300 came to my mind. Could you use $300?" If it had been possible, I would have reached through that phone to hug his neck. "Yes," I replied, "but I need some money today and you're in Florida." "That's no problem," he said, "I'll call the bank in Mt. Sterling and have them take $300 out of my account and put it in yours. Give me a few minutes and you can write a check on your own account." I checked with the bank in about thirty minutes and the money was in my account.

I learned from this experience that there are no limits to which God will go to care for our needs if we have faith in him.

"Now unto Him who is able to do exceeding abundantly beyond all that we ask or think . . ."

(Ephesians 3:20)

A BUILDER OF BUILDINGS
by Paul

After we organized the church where we are still serving, God began to do many miraculous things to bring the building into existence.

We had bought land with an old farm house on it, and so, we began meeting in the old house. One day, before I thought it was time to start building a new church building, one of the men of the congregation decided it was time to start. He sent his wife by our house with a check for $500 to begin the building fund. After we began our building fund, others began to give gifts. Some of them had never been to one of our services and, for that matter, have not been to one since.

Some time passed and we actually began to build. First, we had to find an architect. We found one who drew our preliminary plans for practically nothing. Then, he told us that we would not need his services any longer. According to him, we could do just fine without him and could save quite a bit of money.

Next, we needed someone with a bulldozer to excavate the land. A man from a neighboring town started attending our services. He was in the coal business and was apparently going bankrupt because of large fines imposed on him by the federal environmental protection agency. When he heard us discussing that we needed someone to dig our basement, he said, "I'll move my equipment down here and dig the basement." In a day or two, his equipment was on our property and he started digging. He soon finished and moved the equipment to a wide spot on the highway just west of our property. The day after he finished his work, his equipment was impounded by the government and moved. This man moved to Florida shortly afterwards. We believe God brought him here just to do that work for us.

Many other unusual things happened. We wanted to put stained glass windows in the building. Normally, they were very expensive but ours cost practically nothing. A man donated some sheets of stained glass. We had frames made and put them together with our own hands. We did not have a particular design in mind. One day, after we had put several of them together, we held one up and it had a cross in the middle. We looked at the other finished ones, and they too had crosses in them. After that, we made sure each one had a cross in it.

The dirt which was to be used to fill in around the foundation was filled in too soon after we had put up the frame. In other words, we got in too much of a hurry. We discovered the next day that the front basement wall had buckled and cracked.

On the day I was scheduled to leave to appear on the 700 Club television program in Virginia Beach, Virginia, to tell about my healing of cancer, I went out to the building site, laid my hands on the wall, and commanded it to come back in place in the name of Jesus! Nothing happened and, disappointed, I left for Virginia.

The next day an engineer came by, stopped, looked at the buckled wall, and told the men, "You will have to dig all the dirt from around the wall, tear out the wall, and start from the beginning. When the engineer left, the men were standing in front of the building discussing what to do. Another man came by, stopped, and said, "Looks to me like you men need a backhoe. I have one I'll go get and be back within an hour and do your work for you. When he came back and started digging, the wall popped right back in place. It was such a miraculous thing the men said, "Look at that! The preacher must be somewhere praying!"

When we got to the point where we needed the dry wall hung, a young woman who attended our church met a young man downtown who was a dry wall hanger and finisher. He moved into the old house on our property to live there until he had done all the work he could do on the dry wall, and then he moved on. We never heard from him again.

A man who was driving by the building site one day felt compelled to stop to see what was going on. I showed him around, telling him what we were doing. He made some very complimentary remarks before leaving. After he had been gone a few minutes, we looked up and there he was again. He had driven a few miles down the road when he felt like God spoke to him to give us an offering. He gave us $500.

And so, God put together the building. We believe He said to us, "Upon this hill I will build my church . . ."

"So we built the house of the Lord and finished it . . ."
(I Kings 6:9)

MEAL TICKETS
by Paul

When I was a senior in high school, I won a scholarship to study civil engineering at the University of Kentucky. After attending U.K. for a year, I decided engineering was not for me because God had other plans for my life.

After a series of interesting events , I surrendered my life to the Lord with a promise to be whatever He wanted me to be. Soon, I gave up my engineering scholarship and enrolled in an expensive, private, Baptist college with the intentions of becoming a minister. There was practically no money to pay for tuition, books, room and board, and other necessities. By gifts, loans and small grants, my bills miraculously got paid.

In order to help the ministerial students, the college allowed us to charge a certain number of meal tickets to use when we ate in the college dining room. The meal tickets each cost $10 I was only allowed to charge eight tickets. One time, I received a letter from the treasurer stating that I had reached my limit. I would not be allowed to charge any more until those tickets were paid for. When the last ticket was about gone, I decided to go to the treasurer's office to see if I could charge just one more. The answer was, "No."

I went for a few days without food. I ate just snacks that were lying around the dorm and drank water. Finally, when I couldn't take it any longer, I went back to the treasurer's office to beg them to let me have just one more meal ticket.

When the office worker began to look up my records, I knew I was fighting a lost cause. "I'll just pack up and go home," I thought.

Soon, the clerk returned with a smile on her face and a meal ticket in her hand. "Mr. Prather," she said, "someone has come into this office and paid $80 on your bill! You can charge eight more meal tickets as you need them." Even though she was an older woman and I was just a kid, I could have pulled her from behind that counter and given her a big hug. I went running out of that office and headed for the lunch room - - to eat.

I found out later who did this, but since he wanted it to be an anonymous gift, I didn't mention the incident to him for many years. I am so grateful to this fellow student for providing for my needs in such a trying time.

I learned that our Father will use whomsoever He pleases to care for his children. He used a small lad's lunch to feed five thousand.

"And ordering the multitude to recline on the grass, He took the five loaves and the two fish . . . He blessed the food and gave them to the disciples, and the disciples gave to the multitudes, and they ate and were satisfied . . . and there about five thousand men who ate, aside from the women and children." (Matthew 14:19-21)

IT'S OCTOBER AGAIN
by Paul

Nearly every month we have an opportunity to trust God to get us through the month financially. Because October is my birthday month, car insurance, licenses, taxes, property insurance, and other unforeseen expenses come due. It usually is an extremely trying month for us.

One October, when we stopped to look at what would be due that month, we were overwhelmed. We had more bills due than we had income---not counting what we needed for food, gas, and incidentals. We needed an extra $2000. Looking at things from a purely human viewpoint, there was no way we could make it. However, we stood on the Bible verse which says, "Your Father knows what you have need of before you ask."

Since my birthday is on the fourth of the month, I began to get early birthday cards from various people. In almost every card, there was a small amount of money. One friend came to our house with a check for several hundred dollars. Some of the church people held a birthday party for me. It was supposed to be just cake and ice cream--no gifts. However, church people do not always listen to instructions. Some of them brought small gifts. Others brought cards with cash or checks.

Two of the church ladies decided to have a yard sale on the front yard of the church during 'Court Days in Mount Sterling' which is a county wide flea market. They asked me if I wanted to put out some stuff to sell. I didn't want to do it because I didn't want to carry things out and in. They said they would do it for me. I said I didn't want to have to sit around and sell what I put out. They said for me to price my merchandise and they would sell it for me. Every excuse I offered, they countered with some reason why I should let them do this for me. It must be noted that we had not told anyone about our needs. These women were doing this as an act of goodness. We (they) made more than $200 just for me.

One day I saw a man who knew we had been in the baseball card business. He asked me if we still had the showcase we had while we were in business. We did. He came and bought it and this brought in another $200.

Cathi, our daughter and partner in the baseball card business, went to Court Days in Mt. Sterling where she started a conversation with a baseball card dealer. She sold him the rest of our cards. Chalk up some more cash.

When the month was over, I sat down to figure how much money it had cost us to live during that particular October. Our expenses, not counting food, gasoline, and incidentals were several hundred dollars more than my normal income. We had not told one person our needs. We just told the Father. At the end of the month, all our bills were paid and we had a little left over. Besides being able to give a tithe to the church on all that had come in, we even had money to give to other people.

This was truly a miracle made up of several small miracles. I believe in miracles, small and large. I have learned from this and other miracles which God has performed: don't box God in. Let Him do it His way.

"Is anything too hard for the Lord?"
(Genesis 18:14)

GOD'S TIMING IS PERFECT
by Alice

I like cars and for some reason I liked the looks of an AMC Pacer. One day a classified ad appeared in the local newspaper--- "Pacer For Sale"---and since I needed a little runabout car, I called the number and asked some questions about it. It was at a price I could afford, and the owner wanted to sell it pretty badly so we made a deal.

I brought my Pacer home to clean it up, which was another experience in itself. I found condoms in the door pockets and the glove compartment--I guess the owner wanted to be ready in case a need arose. But since I wasn't expecting to need them, I threw them out along with the dirt. I washed the car, polished it and thought it looked really spiffy. I also learned that other people didn't share my love for a Pacer and I got teased about it looking like a "bug and a bubble," and the teasing was often followed with guffaws. I still liked my little car. It got me to work and the store. That was what I needed it for anyway.

Cars eventually need repairs, and the day came when my Pacer needed tires in a bad way. At that time in our lives, new tires would have worked a real financial hardship on us. When a man in our church found out I needed tires, he asked what size my Pacer took. I told him and he said he thought he had some tires that size under his house. He had wondered what he was going to do with them.

You guessed it. They fit perfectly.

Talk about a miracle for me! I needed tires and this man

had them stored in a dry place. Since he had no idea what he was going to do with them anyway, he gave them to me.

He told us that a few days later a man wanted to buy those tires from him. But it was too late, God had them in "lay-a-way" for me-----free!

God's timing is perfect.

"... *for your Father knows what you need, before you ask Him.*"

(Matthew 6:8)

THE SOURCE OF MY SUPPLY
by Alice

Sometimes I forget just who is the source of my supply. Most of the time I think my job is my source. After all, why else would I work? But our jobs are just instruments God uses sometimes to get his work done. Other times, He uses whatever and whomsoever He chooses.

For instance, last year I realized I was qualified to move up where I worked to a higher rank of secretary. I began to investigate the matter and was given instructions on how to go about getting promoted. I was told not to even suggest it last year because money was too tight but to wait until this year, write a letter, and have my bosses write letters requesting a higher position for me---after all, I had been doing the work of the higher classification for years.

Then, I was told to hang in there. A new committee was being formed and when that committee was completed, I would be notified of the time when they would meet and I could meet with them to present my case. Finally, the day arrived. Five employees came to this meeting. All of us were sure we deserved more money. A couple of them performed duties that didn't fit their titles at all.

One by one, we were called in to face the committee of 12 to 15 people. We were asked generic questions like, "How long have you worked for the system?" And "Why do you think you need a change in title?" This took about 10 minutes each and, then, they were finished with us. We were told to call the chairman of the committee the next day to find out the results of the meeting.

All of us were turned down except one employee; her title was changed to fit her job, but the raise she received was very small. I went to talk to the head man to ask what I would have to do to get the rank I deserved. He told me in a roundabout way that he couldn't override the committee. He wasn't impressed that my job was so monumental that it would take a full-time employee and a half-time employee to keep the job humming as it should. I learned from that conversation that the committee was formed to get people like me off his back anyway. Whatever the committee recommended to the board was what would be passed and he wouldn't have to deal with any of it.

I went back to work the next day discouraged. I decided to continue to do my work, but to relax a little, too, and take time to smell the roses. I would take time to talk to a student who needed someone to listen and if all the paper work took longer to complete--so be it.

In the meantime, my husband and I received a sizable love offering from a friend in Colorado. Just a few short days later, we received another love offering. When I added those together and compared the total to the amount of the raise I would have received, I learned that the Lord was making it up to me another way. In those few short days we had already received enough to cover over two-thirds of the year's raise I might have received.

The message that came to me loud and clear was: the Lord is the source of my supply. My place of employment is not. Whether I am appreciated by my bosses or not, my heavenly Father cares for me. So it's okay . . . I'll go ahead and do my job and smile because the One who's in charge of all things gave me a raise.

"My God shall supply all your needs according to His riches in glory in Christ Jesus."

(Philippians 4:19)

SECTION 3

SPIRITUAL MIRACLES

WHEN I WAS SAVED
by Alice

I seemed to always be aware of another presence even when I was a very small child, but I had no way of really explaining what it was. I was a sensitive child, intending to do what was right all the time after I got past the early training years. I wanted to be saved in our country Baptist church when I was about eight but my granny said I couldn't because I hadn't yet reached the age of "accountability," which was 13, according to her. We all usually did what Granny said. I would see other children go forward in our services and "get saved" and I would cry joy tears for them and sad tears for me because I couldn't go.

When I was a child, church and school could mix. We had visiting missionaries, a man and a woman, who came to our rural two-room school with a folding, portable organ. They taught us songs we had never heard before and told us Bible stories---right in the school. Can you imagine that? When the church had a revival, the whole school turned out for the daytime services. We walked out the road to the church, filed inside, and took our places on the hard, wooden, homemade benches.

At first I liked to go because I got to take two pennies and go inside the country store my grandparents owned to buy two flower-shaped suckers or one sucker and one piece of bubble gum. But one day the service really opened up into an evangelistic service and almost everyone in the whole school went forward on the invitation, including me. They all seemed to be standing up saying they had been saved--except me. I didn't feel any differently and everybody prayed over me until they were worn out. I was getting pretty frustrated myself. Finally, in desperation, I said, "Lord, why can't I be saved?" Suddenly I lit up on the inside, just like someone had turned my light on. I knew something wonderful had happened to me. I was the happiest 13-year-old girl anyone had ever seen.

I, no doubt, belonged to the Lord all along, but I just came into the realization of it that day. I felt like a new person. I began to read my Bible every day and to talk with my friends about what had happened.

When you know you've met the Lord, you become a changed person.

". . .*Believe on the Lord Jesus Christ, and you shall be* saved. . . "

(Acts 16:31)

BAPTIZED IN THE HOLY SPIRIT
by Paul

When I was a young man, I prepared myself to be an educator. I had also felt a call of God on my life to preach. I attended a Christian college where I took all the Bible courses I could fit into my schedule. Finally, I graduated with a major in sociology and minors in Bible and history. I worked and went to school at night, on Saturday, and in the summer to get my teacher's certificate.

For years I taught school and pastored small churches. Eventually, I enrolled in Miami University in Oxford, Ohio, where I received my master's degree in guidance and counseling. A few months before I received that degree I was employed by a small Baptist college to teach sociology and be dean of students. To satisfy the call on my life to preach, I also did supply work for churches who needed someone to fill in while their pastor was away, or who had no pastor.

I set out to make myself a success in the field of education. I felt I was doing a good job as dean. The president often complimented me with remarks like, "You are the best, and, "I don't know what we would do without you!" He promoted me to vice president for student life. However, that president resigned and soon there was a new administration. The new president was a fine man and a very dedicated Christian but we had some philosophical differences. At the end of his first year I resigned to take a job as a professor but that didn't help the situation, so I resigned from the college.

I was already an interim pastor of a large rural church. After my resignation at the college, I became full-time pastor. About a year later, when I could not get them to do what I wanted them to do, I resigned in a fit of anger. No one would invite me to preach, so I ended up getting a teaching job in the seventh grade in a small public school.

Since I had been promoted to vice president of the college the year before I resigned, it was humiliating for me to end up teaching the seventh grade. I felt that everyone was against me and there was no way out. I became really paranoid. I would smile and joke around all day, then cry and pray all night. I was driving my wife, my children, and myself crazy.

One day when the entire family was out of the house, I went to our bedroom to pray. Actually, it was a time of crying and whining before God. I cried out to God. "Lord, You have to do something for me! I can't go on like this!" Suddenly, a great outpouring of the Holy Spirit came upon me. I jumped up from the floor, began to shout and praise the Lord through my tears and ended up running around the room like a wild man. It was absolutely the greatest spiritual experience I had ever had.

Needless to say, it changed my life. The paranoia was gone, as was the other emotional and psychological junk I had picked up. In their place was a new-found joy, a peace beyond understanding, a new love for my family, and a new power in preaching that I did not know existed.

After extensive reading, praying, and studying the Bible, I concluded that I had had a "Pentecostal experience"--I had been baptized in the Holy Spirit! It was a life changing time. I have never been like I was before this happened.

I learned from this experience that there are many

wonderful things the Lord has for us if we will empty ourselves and trust Him to supply all our needs, even spiritual and emotional ones.

"You shall be baptised with the Holy Spirit . . ."
(Acts 1:8)

TONGUES
by Paul

One of the hardest things for me to accept about the Charismatic/Pentecostal movement was "speaking in tongues." God did several things to show me that tongues are for today. I will share three of the most remarkable of these.

Our daughter, Cathi, had a friend who had grown up in the state of New York. They had met while both of them worked at the Grand Canyon. This friend came to visit us and went to church with us. She was not an active Christian, but had attended a Greek Orthodox church. She visited one service at our church in which a man spoke in tongues. After we got home from church, Cathi asked her how she liked the service. She said she was surprised to hear someone speak in Greek and wondered where he learned it. Her mother was Greek so she knew the language. The man later told her he did not speak Greek, did not know Greek, and did not know he was speaking in Greek.

After he had spoken in tongues, the interpretation came for what he had spoken. This young woman said the man had spoken clearly in Greek and the interpretation was perfect. It was part of the Greek Orthodox liturgy with which she was familiar. She became a Christian and received the baptism in the Holy Spirit.

On another occasion, I was preaching and ministering in a meeting in Charlestown, Indiana. In one service a large line of people came forward for prayer. One of these was a young man in his late teens or early twenties. I began to pray for him in English and then, continued to pray for him in tongues. He was touched mightily by the Lord.

After the service a woman walked up to speak with me. "Where did you learn German?" she asked. I told her I did not know the German language and asked her why she asked. "Because, she said, when you prayed for that young man in tongues you were praying in perfect German." She also said the interpretation was exactly right. She was from a German family who spoke German in the home

When I first spoke in tongues, I had only one word--*Shaundi*. I did not know what it meant nor where it came from. However, I kept saying, "*Shaundi, shaundi, shaundi,*" especially when I wanted to praise God. Often when I did not expect it, this word would just seem to float out of my mouth. One day I was reading a book by a minister in Texas. In his book he said the first word of his prayer language was "*Shaundi.*" He also spoke that word many times when he was praising God. On a trip to Indonesia, he heard a native say, "*Shaundi.*" He found out it meant, O, Most High God. He had actually been praising God in another real language. I, too, had been praising God in an Indonesian language I did not know existed. This was a blessed experience for me.

God taught me that He is fluent in all the world's languages, as well as heavenly languages.

"And they were all filled with the Holy Spirit and began to speak with other tongues, as the Spirit was giving them utterance." (Acts 2:4)

I CAN'T BELIEVE
IT HAPPENED TO ME
by Alice

Having been born and reared in a certain denomination, I grew up thinking that speaking in tongues was disgusting--that is, what little I had even heard about it. I thought that if there was such a thing, only weird fanatics would be found doing it. I was married to a preacher of the same denomination and together we didn't really know enough about it to discuss it intelligently.

Then, after twenty-some years of marriage, our lives took an abrupt turn. We didn't ask for it, never thought it would happen or could happen, but it did. After a turn of events---job disappointments, Paul's baptism in the Holy Spirit, a move to another small town, Paul's healing of terminal cancer---just to mention a few, we found ourselves not too well thought of in our beloved denomination. We were on the outside looking in and we hardly realized what had happened. We certainly had not planned it. Old friends no longer acted like they were glad to see us. In fact, Paul saw old friends actually cross the street to keep from speaking to him. However, through all that was happening, we saw many who were learning, along with us, that there was a deeper walk, something more--something we never knew existed. It was wonderful. We couldn't wait to get together to tell what we had learned and what we had seen God do since the last time we met.

Still, through the good things we were experiencing I,

particularly, was seeing a lot of things about which I was skeptical. My little Baptist ears had never heard someone speak in tongues. Nor had I ever seen anyone fall under the power of the Holy Spirit, sing with their eyes closed, or sing songs in church services that made you want to clap your hands and dance. People were acting wild in church and I couldn't handle a lot of it. I didn't even want to handle it. Sometimes I felt like saying, "Get me out of here!

God is so good to me---He knows I have to be shown some things. I don't just fall for any thing that comes down the pike. But I began to soften and one night in a service, I felt the desire to speak in tongues--if it were possible for me. So I went forward in the service and asked the speaker to pray for me. As Paul and I drove away that night, I began to feel a few strange words coming to my mind. One of them was "*shalom*," a word that is common to me now but was not common to me at that time.

One day I was shopping in a downtown department store. As I passed the jewelry counter, my eyes fell on a key chain with the word "Shalom" on it. I could hardly believe what I was seeing---it was a revelation to me. This meant I had not dreamed up an imaginary word. I learned it was a Hebrew word meaning "peace." My curiosity grew and I know now it was the Holy Spirit leading me to go to Paul's study and find his Hebrew dictionary.

I began to try to find the words I had spoken as they had sounded phonetically to me. When I couldn't find them, I began to break those words into what seemed to be syllables. Only they weren't syllables, they were Hebrew words. I found all the words I had been given. They were words of edification---words of peace, prosperity, joy. I didn't, and still don't, know Hebrew, but God let me learn the meaning of those words to show me that this is all real, that it is for today, and that it's okay and to be desired. Why do I have to have things proved to me? And why does He love me so much that He takes all that time to prove Himself to me? I don't know, but, oh, I'm so glad He does!

"And I say to you, ask, and it shall be given to you; seek, and you shall find; knock, and it shall be opened to you."
(Luke 11:9)

SLAIN IN THE SPIRIT
by Paul

Some of the practices within the Charismatic / Pentecostal movement caused me to do a lot of soul-searching and hunting for Scriptural verification. One of these was the phenomenon of being "slain in the Spirit" in which people collapse on the floor when someone who is highly anointed by the Lord prays for them. My former denomination referred to this practice condescendingly as "rolling in the floor." Hence, those who practiced this were called "holy rollers." It was not a term of endearment and, therefore, caused me much mental anguish after I left my old church and became a "Charismatic."

The first experience we had of seeing people slain in the Spirit was at a meeting in Lexington, Kentucky. We attended a meeting where a successful businessman I did not know was giving his testimony. After he had spoken, he invited people who wanted a touch from the Lord to come forward for prayer. He was touching them very lightly and each one was falling on the floor like they had fainted. Several continued to lie on the floor for quite some time, sometimes speaking in a language I did not understand.

Some of them were people I knew from our hometown. We were sitting far from the speaker in the back of the room. I decided to go up front to see what was happening. I wanted to make sure my friends were not being hypnotized. When I got near the front of the auditorium, the speaker called me over to pray for me. I had made up my mind that I would not fall on the floor if he prayed for me. However, when he prayed for me and touched me ever so gently, I fell like a sack of potatoes. I couldn't get up!

Alice left her seat in the back to come to help me get up, but we just had to wait until the Power released me. When I finally got up off the floor, the speaker had me start praying with him. The ones I prayed for also began to fall.

Since that time, I have seen many people slain in the Spirit and, for the most part, I believe this is a valid experience. By the way, I prefer to call it "falling under the power of God."

Once, when several of us were praying for people in one of our hometown churches, a young woman came forward for prayer. She was wearing high heeled shoes. When she was prayed for, she fell under the power of God. While she was lying in the floor, I looked at the place where she had been standing. There, to my amazement, her shoes stood perfectly in place exactly where she had been standing. It looked as if the power of God had just lifted her up and placed her gently on her back. Many people witnessed this unusual act of God.

God taught me through these experiences that He can demonstrate His power anyway He chooses, whether we believe it or not.

> *"And when I saw Him, I fell at His feet like a dead man . . . "* (Revelation 1:17)

STRANGERS GET
A WORD FROM GOD
by Paul

Several years ago, I was traveling from Western Kentucky back home to Mt. Sterling, Kentucky. I had heard of a truck stop in Elizabethtown that served delicious vegetable soup and cornbread. Being a connoisseur of soup, I decided to stop for a bowl and some of that good cornbread.

When I went in, all the tables were taken so I took a seat at the counter on a stool. While I was eating, I noticed a couple sitting to my back in a booth near the wall. I wasn't even thinking on spiritual matters. I was thinking about food. But then, I heard the voice of the Lord whisper to me, "I have a word for you to deliver to that couple!"

After thinking and silently praying for a few minutes, I went over to the couple. "Are you folks open for a word from the Lord?" I asked. A bewildered look came on their faces, but finally the man looked up and said, "Well, yes, if it is from the Lord."

I gave them what I felt the Lord told me to say and got out of there as quickly as possible because the expressions on their faces were intimidating. When I got to my car, I looked around and there stood the woman. She asked, "Sir, who are you?"

"It doesn't make any difference who I am. If the word I gave you was from the Lord, just receive it and praise Him for it," I replied. "If it wasn't, just forget it."

"Sir, if you had known all about us, you couldn't have spoken anything that would have been more appropriate," she said. Again she asked me who I was and I told her the same thing, "It doesn't really matter who I am, just take the word as from the Lord!"

By this time I was getting in my car. "Are you an angel?" she asked. Assuring her that I was not did not convince her.

Later, we heard from a friend who heard her tell the story in a church service in Radcliffe, Kentucky. Through this friend we learned that she took down my license number and had it checked out by the state police. She had evidently copied the wrong number because the police could not find out who I was. I have never contacted them nor have they contacted me.

Another time, Alice and I and another couple were in a restaurant in Indiana on a Sunday after I had spoken in their church. A young couple with two children came into the restaurant. I felt the same moving of the Spirit to give them a word from the Lord. I went over to their table and had essentially the same conversation with them that I'd had with the other couple. I gave them the word the Lord had given me for them. The woman began to cry and the man looked bewildered. I got back to my table as quickly as possible. After a few minutes had passed, the woman came over to our table and said, "I am sorry I burst out crying but this morning we really needed guidance. We prayed before we went to church that we would hear a word from the Lord today and we didn't hear from Him. You can imagine how we felt when we came in here and you gave us the very word we needed after we were feeling that God had not answered our prayer. Thank you for being obedient!"

I learned from these and other experiences that you can't

expect God to always do things the same traditional ways every time. Also, I learned God is always present and can meet us where our needs are, even in a restaurant when our minds are not particularly on Him.

In Acts 8:26-39 *Phillip was led by the Spirit to go to the Ethiopian eunuch whom he had never met, answer his questions, and preach Jesus unto him. The eunuch received Jesus as his Saviour and was baptised.*

WORDS
OF PERSONAL PROPHECY
by Paul

Once about five years ago, I was ministering in a revival meeting in a church between Campbellsville and Columbia, Kentucky. One night the Lord began to move mightily through me in the gift of personal prophecy, or perhaps it could be better described as words of knowledge and encouragement. From the Spirit within you, you suddenly know things about someone or a situation of which you have no knowledge.

Here are two of those personal words:

The Lord moved on me to give a man I did not know this prophecy: "You will get electricity in your house within the next six months. It will not cost you anything." I found out that this man had been trying for quite a long time to get electricity to his house. He and his family lived a long way from the nearest neighbor who had electricity. Therefore, the cost of getting power to his house was astronomical. He could not afford to have it done.

Later that night after I had given the prophecy, the pastor told me, "You had better be right on this one! Everyone here knows the circumstances and knows it will take a miracle to bring it to pass!"

I'm glad to report that the prophecy was from God and not from me. A few weeks later I learned that someone had begun to build a house near this man's property and needed a right of way across his property. They offered him electricity free for allowing them to come across his land. The man to whom I had prophesied got electricity in his house at no cost to him, and he got it in less than six months.

In the same meeting, I was praying for the children who were in the service. I felt the anointing of the Lord to prophesy to two young boys about nine or ten years old. The prophecy was, "You two boys are being raised up to serve in the army of the Lord. You are not going to be privates, you are both going to be captains in His army." I did not know these children and only casually knew their parents.

The next day the pastor along with some other members of his church and I went to the home of one of them where we were told that these boys often played "army." They would argue with each other about who was going to be the private and who was going to be the captain. It was very interesting that God spoke to them in terms which they could understand! This 'miracle' blew my mind!

I learned from these two incidents that God knows all about us. He meets us where we are, and speaks to us in terms we can understand.

"Now there are varieties of gifts, but the same Spirit . . . For to one is given the word of wisdom . . . to another the word of knowledge . . . to another faith . . . to another gifts of healings . . . to another the effecting of miracles . . . and to another prophecy . . ."

(from I Corinthians 12:4-10)

SWEET AROMA
by Paul

Several ministers and I were involved in a great meeting in Charlestown, Indiana, where many mighty works were taking place.

One night during the meeting, I was standing on the front row getting ready to go to the pulpit to preach. We were finishing an anointed time of worship and praise and had our heads bowed and our eyes closed. I smelled a strikingly lovely fragrance. It was as if a woman with the most aromatic perfume I had ever smelled just walked in front of me. I took a deep breath to inhale the aroma. It was absolutely the sweetest fragrance I had ever smelled. I opened my eyes to see who had walked by. There was no one there. I looked to see who was spraying the perfume. It was like puffs were coming from the altar, but there was no one spraying perfume or air freshener.

I really did not know what was happening. After a few seconds, perhaps a minute or two, I heard the man standing behind me take a deep breath and then let it out. I thought, "He smells it, too." Then, from across the aisle I heard someone else take a deep breath and let it out. People all throughout the church house began to breathe deeply and then to audibly exhale with a long sound, "wheww-w-w-w-w---ah-ah-ah-ah-ah!"

Suddenly, I knew what was happening: The Lord had blessed us with the sweet smelling aroma of Jesus. Everyone present knew we were in the presence of the

Glory of God.

> *"Christ gave himself . . . as a fragrant aroma."*
> (Ephesians 5:2)

HOLY LAUGHTER
by Paul

Today, there is an evangelist who ministers in the phenomenon of holy laughter. Entire congregations burst out in laughter. People whom the evangelist touches break forth in uncontrollable laughter. However, in the earlier days of my ministry, I had never heard of such a thing. My first experience with holy laughter took place in a meeting in which I was preaching in Indiana.

On a particular night in this meeting, I had preached and, as usual, had started to pray for those who had come forward for prayer. One man said to me simply, "I need a touch from the Lord!" I laid hands on him and began to pray. When I did, he began to laugh slightly. I moved on to the next person to pray for her and she began to laugh softly, too. The man I had just prayed for began to laugh louder. The woman joined him. Others, then, began to laugh, some of them loudly. There was such a spirit of laughter in the service, I began to laugh. Before long, practically the whole congregation was laughing. This lasted a long time---so long that my jaws and sides began to hurt. I wanted to quit but I couldn't.

Finally, when the laughter had subsided, people began to give testimonies saying, "While we were laughing, I was healed of _____." Testimonies were heard for all kinds of illnesses. Some said, "When we came in here, I had a headache and now it is gone. I was healed while we were laughing! " Others said the same thing about other aches and pains leaving.

This was one of those unusual things that just blew my denominational mind. We had never seen or heard of anything like this in our denomination. I wondered, "Could this really be from God?" I could find nothing in the Scriptures about this happening anywhere in the New Testament. In the Book of Acts the disciples rejoiced in the Lord but they sang hymns and prayed, no laughter was mentioned.

It seemed to me that laughing was a good catharsis for a wounded and broken spirit. As I began to see this happening in other services and witnessing people being healed and set free from bondage, I concluded this, too, was from the Lord.

"A merry heart doeth good like a medicine . . ."
(Proverbs 17:22)

DAVID'S CAR
by Paul

For a few years, I taught a Bible study in the basement of a Methodist church near Somerset, Kentucky, which was about 100 miles from my home.

One night when I was scheduled to go to this Bible study, I did not have the money to buy gasoline to make the trip. I felt God say in my spirit, "You start and I will provide for your expenses." I left home with an empty gas tank and only a few coins in my pocket.

I drove across town where I had to pass a small community grocery store. They did not sell gasoline at this market but I felt the strongest inner urge to stop there. I stopped and went in. When I entered the store, there was a man who said, "I have been looking for you today. The Lord told me to give you $20." That was enough in those days to buy a tank of gasoline and have money left to buy food. That night the group felt led to take an offering for me and, so, God did exactly what He had promised and more.

At that same Bible study group, David, a young aspiring preacher who drove about 90 miles round trip each week to attend, came up and asked us to pray for him to receive a better car. His car was in really bad shape, being partially tied together with wire. The tail pipe was gone and it needed new tires, among other things. The people gathered around him and we prayed according to his request.

David had really latched on to the faith and confession message. When he got home, he parked his car in the driveway as usual. But, when people came to visit, he would ask them, "Did you see my new car as you came in? Of course, the answer would be negative and he would reply, "Well, it's there. I can see it by faith." He kept this up for several months. Some of his family thought he had flipped out and actually talked about having him committed for observation.

In the meantime, a lady who did not know anything about all this started attending the Bible study. She was a widow who had recently married a widower. They both had good automobiles. However, they only used one car. The other one was parked in a garage. She began to feel the urge to give it to someone. Finally, one night after she had attended the Bible study, she talked to her husband about giving the car away. He said, "It's your car! Give it away if you want to!" She began to pray about to whom to give it. She had also noticed David's car and could not help but see what shape it was in. She decided to give it to him.

At the next meeting of the group after her decision, she called David aside and asked, "David, could you use a better car?" He began to shout and praise God, especially when he learned that the car was practically new and had been kept in a garage for months.

David took the car home in a few days and parked it in his driveway. Then, when those same people who thought he might need to be committed came to visit, he would say, "Now, did you see my new car as you came in?" The answers were quite different than they were before.

"All things are possible to him who believes."
(Mark 9:23)

PRAISING BABY
by Paul

A few months ago a man and his wife from Georgia visited in our church services. She was obviously several months pregnant. In fact, I learned the baby was due at any time.

When our prayer time came, she and her husband came forward for prayer. Her prayer request was quite simple. She wanted us to pray for an easy and safe delivery. I did not know that she was going to have a home delivery with a midwife. We prayed according to her request and, then, a word came to them from the Lord: "This baby is an anointed child. It is so anointed that when it is born it will come forth out of the womb with its hands raised praising the Lord." The couple returned to their home in Georgia but did not tell anyone what the word was. Within a month the baby was born.

The child's grandmother, who is a member of our church, went to Georgia to be with her daughter during the birth. After the child was born, one of the women who helped with the birthing told the grandmother, "You should have seen that baby. She had her little hands up and was waving them like she was praising the Lord." She did not know about the prophesy the parents had received while they were in Kentucky. Like Mary, the mother of Jesus, this child's mother had pondered these things in her heart but had told no one.

"And Mary treasured up all these things, pondering them in her heart."

(Luke 2:19)

AN EXCELLENT WIFE
FOR OUR SON
by Alice

"An excellent wife, who can find?
For her worth is far above jewels.
The heart of her husband trusts in her,
And he will have no lack of gain.
She does him good and not evil
All the days of her life."
(Proverbs 31: 10,11,12)

When our son was growing up, he was a good student, artistic, loved to read, and played football for nine years. The high school years came and he seemed to be popular with the teachers and students. His teachers always told us good things about him and his friends elected him "Mr. This" and "Mr. That." He never seemed to have trouble getting dates once his nerve allowed him to ask a girl out. Girls don't know this, but boys have to work up the nerve to ask a girl for a date. They aren't always the "cool dudes" they want everybody to think they are.

He dated some cute girls. Most of them were lively, popular, and liked to have money spent on them---who doesn't? College came and there were more girls who seemed to be the same type as the high school girls, only older. He wasn't living a Christian life at this time and he wasn't looking for a mate for the future either.

However, the time came when he didn't know what course his life should take. He felt it necessary to drop out of college for a while until he could figure it all out. In the meantime, God moved mightily in his life and he knew what direction he would be going. He would be in some type of ministry.

Our daughter, Cathi, had a friend whose name was Renee. For some reason Cathi had not mentioned to Renee that her brother was now on the local scene. He had not gone to the school Cathi and Renee attended. He had been away at college. She came to church with Cathi and spotted this guy in the service. She later said she had thought to herself, "There's the boy I'm going to marry," without even knowing who he was. She was really shocked when she learned he was Cathi's brother.

When I learned she was interested in him, I was sure he wouldn't ask her out because she didn't quite fit the mold of the others he had dated. Renee was unspoiled, calm, sweet, and a cute girl from a different world because she had been reared in a Pentecostal home. That was something, because our lives had taken a dramatic turn and we were moving in the realm of Pentecostalism, too.

He asked her out. I said, "He'll never ask her out the second time." But he did. In a short time we began to see they were getting serious---real serious! Renee had been voted Miss Montgomery County Fair Queen. If she married, she would lose her crown---her first runner-up would have to finish her reign. She gave it up without a second thought. They were married in about five months from the first date to the wedding date.

Paul and Renee have been married 16 years now. She wasn't thrilled with the idea of being a minister's wife (as I wasn't), but the Lord knew she was exactly what he needed and He brought them together. If we had gone looking for a wife for him, we couldn't have found a more perfect mate. They allow each other freedom to be themselves. He is a writer, teacher and minister now. She has allowed him freedom to spend time reading and writing while she and their son, John, did their own thing. She has worked and helped support them financially while Paul finished his college work and got his career going. She did all that without complaining.

God knew what He was doing all along. He allowed Paul to *"find an excellent wife!"*

APPARITIONS BRING
GOD'S MESSAGES
by Paul

At least two times in my life, I have been given messages from beings who appeared to me at times when I really needed to know what I should do.

One of these appearances occurred while we lived in northeastern Ohio where I was a pastor and public school teacher. A multitude of problems in this church made this pastorate very difficult.

Needless to say, I had a very difficult time adjusting to all the confusion. I was having a lot of difficulty sleeping, eating, and functioning in general. One night while I was sound asleep, I was awakened by the feeling of a presence in our room. When I completely awakened, I saw a man standing at the foot of our bed. He spoke to me. "Leave the church. Get your family out of here. Don't preach at _____ Church again," he said and vanished. I spent the rest of the night reading the Bible, walking the floor, and praying. I decided to resign the church and move back to Kentucky.

I didn't preach at that church again. I went to the midweek service the next night and resigned. By the time I took two weeks vacation which I had coming to me, we had made arrangements to move. I believed God had spoken to me through the person who had appeared in my room that night.

Another time I was having a very hard time trying to decide about some doctrinal matters. One night during this period, I had gone to bed but was not asleep. I was tossing and turning when I looked at the foot of the bed. There stood my mother who had been dead for a few years. She spoke to me, "Son, read the third chapter of Zephaniah." Before I really comprehended what she had said, she was gone. "Come back," I yelled, "What did you say?" She appeared again and said, "Read the third chapter of Zephaniah." Then, she was gone again. I immediately went to sleep with a wonderful peace I had never had before.

The next morning as soon as I could get my eyes open, I got my Bible, hunted for the Book of Zephaniah, and read the third chapter over and over again. Before this happened, I hardly knew the Book of Zephaniah existed.

Here is some of what I read:

> Do not be afraid, O Zion; do not let your
>   hands fall limp,
> The Lord your God is in your midst,
> A victorious warrior.
> He will exult over you with joy,
> He will be quiet in His love,
> He will rejoice over you with shouts of joy...
> Behold, I am going to deal at that time with
>   all your oppressors...
> At that time I will bring you in, even at the
>   time when I gather you together.
> Indeed, I will give you renown and praise
>   among all the peoples of the earth.
> When I restore your fortunes before your
>   eyes, says the Lord."
>
> (Zephaniah 3:16-20)

When we seek the Lord and His will for our lives, He will make sure we find that for which we are looking.

"Ask and it shall be given to you; seek, and you shall find; knock, and it shall be opened to you. For everyone who asks receives, and he who seeks finds, and to him who knocks it shall be opened."

(Matthew 7:8-9)

". . .a vision appeared to Paul in the night, a certain man of Macedonia was standing and appealing to him and saying, 'Come over to Macedonia and help us.' And when he had seen the vision, immediately we sought to go to Macedonia, concluding that God had called us to preach the gospel to them." (Acts 16: 9-10)

PRAY FOR LOVING IN-LAWS?
by Alice

When I was about seventeen years old, occasionally I began to think about my future. I intended to marry. All girls knew marriage was in their futures back then, and I was no different. I just didn't think it would happen within the next year or two.

Somehow, though, I understood the importance of having in-laws who would love me, so I began to pray prayers like this: "Lord, when I get married, please let my husband's family love me." I've always thought this was a strange prayer for a seventeen-year-old girl to pray when I really didn't understand much about prayer. It was also strange because most girls would have been praying for a husband with no thought of in-laws.

Maybe it was because my parents and I had always lived with my paternal grandparents. My mother and grandmother had a strained relationship. I don't think my grandmother disliked my mother any more than she would have disliked any girl who took her only living son "away from her." It wasn't a real bad situation but the strain was always there. I suppose I must have heard other people talk about in-law problems. Anyway, I believe the Lord directed me to begin praying about my future. After all, I didn't have to pray. I could have just let it all happen.

Two short years later, I met the real man for me. Then, one-by-one, and two-by-two, I began to meet his family. Those were the meetings when they sized me up, and I them. Then, we began to feel free enough to talk. Soon, we could even laugh about a few things --all leading up to good relationships. As the years passed, I learned to love them and accept them as the large family I'd never had.

Paul's mother and I were always close. We could talk, shop, or work together without a cross word. Once, one of Paul's sisters said she thought their mother cared more for me than she did her own daughters. Paul's mother was never selfish with me. In fact, she thought I should have everything I wanted whether it was furniture, clothes, or the moon. There were times when Paul and I would disagree about something in front of her. She always came to my defense. She was a well-read woman who always had something interesting to talk about. I enjoyed our friendship very much. There were times when the biblical story of Ruth and Naomi (the daughter-in-law was Ruth who loved her mother-in-law, Naomi) came to my mind. I began to understand how it might be possible for a daughter-in-law to love her mother-in-law so much.

I think our loving God cares for our every need if we will only listen and heed His directions. He wants us to be happy and feel loved and accepted. Sometimes, He directs us to pray for things that seem strange at the time, just as my directions to pray for the love of future in-laws, whom I had never met, seemed strange. Forty-two years later I'm so glad I obeyed.

"To obey is better than sacrifice."
(I Samuel 14:22)

SECTION 4

MISCELLANEOUS MIRACLES

OIL BOTTLE FILLED
by Paul

A few years ago, I was the speaker at a Full Gospel Business Men's Fellowship International meeting in Huntington, West Virginia. After the close of my message a long prayer line was formed. I began praying for each of them and anointing them with oil in the name of Jesus.

I had brought my own bottle of oil which was about two-thirds full. I prayed for people for about 45 minutes. When it seemed that the prayer time was over, the man who was carrying my oil bottle handed it to me. I looked at the bottle. It was full to the brim. I began shouting praises to the Lord. I had prayed for people for a long time and used lots of oil. God had filled the bottle. People who were present began to bring small containers, like the little creamers which were on the tables, to have them filled with the oil. A medical doctor who was sitting on the front row asked if I would like for him to write and sign an affidavit stating he had seen the bottle before we started, and had also seen it after it was filled. However, I felt anyone who would not believe without an affidavit would not believe even with one.

The oil bottle remained full for a long time. However, after some months I accidentally spilled all the oil out of the bottle.

I learned two lessons from this. First, God is God of the little things like little oil bottles.

Then, I learned God will not share His glory with anyone

or anything, even a bottle of oil. He wants us to look to Him for our blessings and as the source of our supply and not to someone or something else. Oil is simply the means He uses in certain circumstances.

"Is any among you sick? Let him call for the elders of the church and let them pray over him, anointing him with oil in the name of the Lord, and the prayer offered in faith will restore the one who is sick, and the Lord will raise him up..."

(James 5:14-15)

A NEW PIANO
by Paul

We started a non-denominational Charismatic church in 1977. We met in various places, such as members' homes, the basement of a union hall, our own front room, and other locations which were available. The musical instruments consisted of whatever was available. Then, in 1978 we purchased the property where we are now located on U.S. 60, three miles west of Mt. Sterling, Kentucky. Soon after we moved into the house on the property we were given an old upright piano.

God sent us a young woman, Judy, to play the piano. About the same time we started making serious plans to build a building to worship in, since we had been meeting for some time in an old farm house on the property we bought, Judy began to pray for a new white baby grand piano for the new building. We all started to believe for a "new white baby grand piano." Someone in the church body really got into the spirit of things and painted the old upright white. This was by no means satisfactory to Judy. She was praying for a new white baby grand piano.

Sometime before this, I had been asked to go to a home to pray for an elderly woman who was confined to her bed. She received a real touch from the Lord and got up and walked for the first time in years. A long time later she passed away. After her death, her son visited one of our church services. As he left that Sunday, he said, "Come and visit me sometime because I want to do something for you in memory of my mother." I had no idea what he had in mind.

In the meantime, our people kept praying for a new white baby grand piano. Judy kept saying, "I can't wait to get in the new building and play on that new white baby grand piano!"

One evening as I was out visiting, I decided to visit the man who had asked me to come by his house. He said, "I want to buy a piano or organ for your new building in memory of my mother." I told him we didn't really need an organ but we had been praying for a new piano. I did not tell him we had been praying for a white baby grand piano. What he had in mind, he told me, was a baby grand piano. Well, I was so excited I went to the phone and called my wife and told her that this man was going to give us a baby grand piano. "Don't forget to tell him we want a white one," she said.

I went back into the room where he was and told him we wanted a white baby grand. The color made no difference to him, so he went the next day and bought us the piano we had prayed for. It cost over $6000.

I found out God really doesn't care very much about colors. We wanted white, so He gave us white. Maybe we don't get what we want because we are not specific enough when we pray. God loves us. His word says, "Delight yourself in the Lord and He will give you the desires of your heart."

"Praise Him with stringed instruments . . ."
(Psalm 150:4)

126

GOD REPAIRS CARS
by Paul

I have seen God do many wonderful things, but I never cease to be amazed at the miraculous little things He does. Three of these are about Him repairing cars.

We were having a special meeting with an out-of-town speaker. A man who attended the services every night started to leave after one of the services. When he went out to get in his car, it wouldn't start. The guest speaker and I were the last ones out of the building. When we got outside, the man had his hood up trying to start the car. We walked over to where he was parked and asked what was wrong. It was too dark to see the motor. Our guest speaker reached his hand under the hood to a place he could not see and said, "Right here is your trouble!"

Someone brought us a flashlight. Guess what? When the owner of the car looked under the hood at the place where the evangelist had told him, there was a loose wire. They repaired it and the car started.

On a Wednesday I had visited my mother in Somerset, Kentucky, ninety miles from our home. On the way back my car started to run irregularly. Eventually, it quit running in Lexington, about thirty-five miles from home. I got out and opened the hood. When I did, steam began to boil out. The car had been overheating for many miles and finally quit running.

Almost immediately after I raised the hood, a pick-up truck pulled up right behind where I had stopped. A very pleasant man got out and asked what the problem was. I told him. He said he thought he could fix it. He went back to his car, rummaged through his tools, and came back with everything he needed to fix the burst hose. He even had some water to put in the radiator. "I think you can get home now," he said. After starting the car to continue my trip, I looked around to thank him and he was gone. I would have seen him if he had passed me--he didn't. I concluded God had sent an angel to guide me on my way. After I got home, a member of our church who was a mechanic found the distributor cap full of water. "There is no way you could have made it home in this car," he said. And, I couldn't have. It was God who brought me home.

The third incident happened to me on a rainy, stormy night when I was about 50 miles from home. My windshield wipers quit. I could not see to drive. I pulled off to the side of the road and prayed. I got out of the van, laid my hands on the wipers, and commanded them to work in the name of Jesus. When I got back into the van and started the motor, the wipers began to work. They worked until I got back home. The next day I took the van to a mechanic who informed me that the wiper motor was burned out and had to be replaced.

These three incidents taught me that God is more powerful than any man made object and He can repair cars when we trust in Him.

"All power is given Me in heaven and earth . . ."
(Matthew 28:18)

THE RAIN STOPS
by Paul

A few years back, I was teaching regularly at the Monday Night Bible Study, then held at Calvary Assembly of God Church in Lexington, Kentucky.

One evening after I started to Lexington, it began to rain in torrents. It rained on me all the way from Mt. Sterling to Lexington. When I got to a shopping center on the outskirts of the city, I thought, "I had better stop here and buy an umbrella. Suddenly, on the inside of me I heard the still small voice of the Lord say, "Why don't you trust me?" "Okay," I said, "but you will have to do one of three things: either stop the rain, find me a place to park close to the church, or put your umbrella over me to keep me from getting wet!" It seems to me that God couldn't care one way or the other about umbrellas, but it really mattered to me that I didn't get wet. I didn't want my new suit spotted with rain.

Just before I arrived at the church, when I was one block away, the rain suddenly stopped. It was like someone had turned off the faucet. When I got to the church, there was an empty parking place right next to the front entrance. As I got out of the car, I looked up to see what was happening. I saw a lot of water dripping from the electric wires and trees.

In the vestibule of the church, a lady had tables of books set up to sell. She looked at me and exclaimed, "How did you get in here without getting wet? There is not a drop of water on you anywhere!" I looked all over myself for a spot of water. There was none! The Lord had done all three things I had asked Him to do: stopped the rain, found a place for me to park, and put His umbrella over me.

I learned from this that the elements are subject to the power of God. Also, I found out that He has a great big umbrella to put over us when we need it!

"Elijah was a man with a nature like ours, and he prayed earnestly that it might not rain; and it did not rain on the earth for three years and six months. And he prayed again, and the sky poured rain. and the earth produced its fruit."
(James 5:17-18)

CHURCH IN NEW MEXICO
WAITS FOR ME
by Paul

One year Alice and I were feeling burned out. We wanted to go to Arizona to see our daughter who was working at the Grand Canyon and, then, on to California. There was one big problem: we didn't have the money. After praying, we decided God wanted us to get away for a while. We felt instructed to start confessing we were going to California in June. We began to make plans and tell everyone we were going . . . but we believed we were not to tell anyone about our financial situation.

At the time, I was teaching a Bible study in Princeton, Kentucky, once a month. When I went to Princeton on the last Monday in May, I told them I would not be there in June because we were going to California on a vacation and to visit relatives. I was careful not to tell them about our financial needs. A few days later, after I returned to our home in Mt. Sterling, Kentucky, I received a letter from one of the women at the Bible study whom I hardly knew at that time. In the letter was a check from this woman with a note attached. It read simply. "I want to be part of your trip to California." The check was for $100. Small amounts of money began to come in from many sources until on the date we intended to leave we had more than enough to make the trip. And, we hadn't told anyone our needs--except the Father!

We started on a Monday and ended up in a little town

near the New Mexico - Arizona border, on the New Mexico side, on a Wednesday night. We were quite tired and not dressed for church, so Alice decided to sleep in. Since I couldn't sleep, I decided to go somewhere to church. I looked in the telephone book and found the name of an Assembly of God church whose services started at 7:00 p.m. However, I got lost on the way there and arrived at the church about 7:20. Since I was so late, I almost did not go in.

After I sat in the car for a few seconds, I spotted a man standing in the glass entrance. I finally decided to go in for the services. When I got to the door, the man said, "Are you a preacher?" I told him I was. "Well, praise the Lord," he said. He explained to me that their pastor was gone to a convention and the person who was to preach that night had not come, so they were without a preacher. The rest of the congregation was in a back room praying for the Lord to send them a preacher. It was this man's job to wait at the door until the preacher arrived and then, notify the rest of them.

I went in and preached. We had a wonderful service and they asked me to stop on the way back home and preach for them again. We did not return home by the same route, so I have never heard from them since.

God is able to put us where He wants us, when He wants us to be there. I remembered the story told in the book of Acts about Phillip being caught up by the Spirit into the wilderness to preach to a man he did not know.

"...And when they came up out of the water, the Spirit of the Lord snatched Phillip away; and the eunuch saw him no more, but went on his way rejoicing."

(Acts 8:39)

PROTECTED FROM THE RAIN
by Paul

One time, at the request of a very good friend, I took my truck to Birmingham, Alabama, to haul some antique furniture she wanted me to sell back to Mt. Sterling, Kentucky. I did not have a topper on the bed of my pick-up. Therefore, we tied plastic over the load to try to protect it in case of rain.

Before I had traveled very far, most of the plastic had blown off the furniture. I stopped several times to try to secure the plastic to the truck and over the furniture. Repeatedly, it continued to blow off. I had planned to return home through Somerset, Kentucky, to take care of some business. Just before I arrived in Somerset, the sky filled with dark clouds. It was obvious to me that a downpour was headed our way. By the time I reached Somerset, sprinkles began to fall. I stopped at a house we owned in Somerset and quickly unloaded the truck, just before the clouds burst. Finally, after a long, hard rain, the sun came out and the skies cleared. I reloaded the truck and again began my trip home.

I had traveled about 30 miles when the skies began to cloud up again. It was obvious that another hard rain was on its way. There was no place to get the truck in the dry and no place to unload. I began to pray, "Lord, please keep the rain away. Please protect these things I am hauling. Lord, these things will be ruined if they get wet. Lord, please do something." The rains came so hard and fast many drivers pulled their cars off the highway because they couldn't see where they were going.

After about 30 minutes of driving in this hard rain, I came to a small town where there was a service station with a large canopy out over the pumps. I pulled the truck under the canopy to get gasoline. As I was putting the gasoline in, I forced myself to glance at the load on the back: it was dry! Water was standing in the truck bed, but the load was completely dry. I drove a few miles farther to the house of some friends and called them to come out to see what had happened. They could hardly believe me when I told them I had driven through the rain because all the materials on the back of my truck were uncovered. The plastic had all blown away but the furniture was completely dry.

I learned there is no end to what God can do. He has an umbrella big enough to cover the load on a pick-up truck.

"Ask and it shall be given you . . ."
(Matthew 7:7)

GOD PROVIDES A WIFE
by Paul

Because my mother had dedicated me to the Lord, He was doing miraculous things for me long before I had any idea what He was doing. One of these was bringing me the right woman to be my wife.

After I really surrendered my life to the Lord, I began to pray for God to send me a wife. I wanted His will to be done. I wanted to find the right girl with whom to spend my life. I felt there was only one person with whom I could be happy. I kept waiting and waiting. I thought maybe God would bring her to me riding in a Rolls Royce. It sure didn't happen that way.

I had a friend who was a farm boy. Living on the farm adjoining his family's farm was a young woman who was highly thought of in the community. Her reputation was impeccable. My friend decided that she and I should go out together. His high praises of her made me think he was right. Finally, I decided to allow him to see if he could fix me up with a date with her. It turned out to be a blind date for me because I didn't know her, even though I often went into the office where she worked. She knew who I was and so it was not really a blind date for her. We went to a revival on our first date---my mother went with us.

After the first date, it was revealed to me in my spirit that this young woman would be my wife. I was so sure of it that I immediately quit dating any other girls and concentrated on her. On the third date I told her I was going to marry her. She laughed. However, I was very serious. I knew she was mine. Somehow, I knew that God had put us together. It was obvious we were meant for each other. We laughed, talked, did lots of fun things together, were constantly in each other's company, and enjoyed life together tremendously. Two months later, she became really bold in confessing her love for me. "If I ever marry anyone, I guess it will be you," she said. But, she added that marriage was way out in the future. We were married in about three more months.

All this happened in the Fall and Winter of 1952-53. She was 19 - I was 22 when we were married in March, 1953. We have been happily married for over 42 years, at this writing. Our lives have been one miraculous event after another.

I have learned from all these years together that life can be sweet when you spend it in the center of God's will with the mate God has chosen just for you.

"Charm is deceitful and beauty is vain, but a woman who loves the Lord, she shall be praised."

(Proverbs 31:30)

HOW WE MET
by Alice

I was a country girl. So, when I finished the eighth grade in the rural two room school, I should have gone to a rural high school. In fact, the big yellow bus passed right by my house. However, my best friend's brothers could go up town to the city high school because their father owned property in the city limits and, of course, my friend would be going there too. She began to talk to me about going to the up town school with her and the more she talked, the better it sounded.

There were two catches, at least. One, we didn't have dependable transportation and, two, my family would have to pay tuition for me to go there, because we didn't own any property in the city limits. But I felt so strongly about going to the city high school that I almost became obsessed with the idea. I began to beg my parents, mainly my mother, to let me please go. I even promised them that some day when I finished high school I would pay them back what they spent. (Of course, I never did.)

There were days when we rode the three miles to school with whoever would let us hitch a ride. There were days when we walked. There were days when we walked part of the way and rode the city bus the rest of the way. Part of the time I paid another student one dollar a week to ride in his Model A Ford. Another friend and my cousin also rode with him. All four of us were farm kids or I might not have understood when he used his car as a truck part of the time by taking out the back seat and hauling milk cans back there. My friend and I were elected to sit on those cans. It seems he should have paid us to ride with him, but the giggles and snickers we enjoyed when we realized how ridiculous we looked and felt, made it worth the dollar we each paid.

By my senior year, I had my driver's license. My dad took pity on me and let me drive the family car. Sometimes he would take us and then come back into town to pick us up. By the time I graduated, I was so weary with it all that college didn't sound a bit good to me. My mother wanted me to go to college but I said I wanted to work a year and then I would go.

Just days before graduation, my English teacher found out I wasn't going to college and told me about a job opening at the local newspaper office. The owners were friends of hers and she said for me to go down to the office and tell them she had sent me. I must have left school that day and stopped at the newspaper office and landed the job, because I remember going home and telling my family what I had done and that I had a new job. My family was the cautious, wait-and-see kind. I still remember how shocked they were, especially my grandmother, when they learned I had taken such a big step and changed jobs without even talking to them about it first.

One day at this newspaper office a young man in a suit came in to put an ad in the paper. A young woman who worked there introduced us. She knew everyone on a first name-basis---in fact, she never forgot a name or a face. He finished his business and left. Occasionally, I would see him in his car and remember that that was Paul Prather. Once my car even fell in behind his going around the town's fountain square and I remember thinking how straight and nice he looked as he drove his car.

My best friend's brothers also knew Paul and, of course, her brother had known me all my life. He got us together for a blind date, except that I knew who I was going out with and the blind date was only "blind" for Paul. When they came to the door to get me, Paul's first words were, "Oh, I know you!" We went to church that night and picked up Paul's mother on the way and took her with us. Paul and I were married five months later. That was over 42 years ago.

Was it just a childish craving that made me want to go to a school that wasn't in my district? Was it just sheer determination that made me keep on going through all I went through to get to that school and back home again? Or was it just luck that made my English teacher tell me about that job opening instead of some other girl?

No, I believe the Lord was leading me all the way. How else would I have met Paul? For financial reasons, he had to drop out of college that year. If he had had the money he would have been away at college and we wouldn't have met anyway. God was working from both sides of our lives to bring us together.

"Thou art the God who works wonders . . ."
(Psalm 77:14)

LITTLE THINGS
by Paul

I have often heard people say, "I wouldn't bother God with little things like that!" I have found out our Father is concerned about little, insignificant things when they can be helpful to us.

At one church where I was pastor we had a rather large amount of playground equipment. Among this equipment was a set of outdoor horseshoes. They were used quite often at picnics, get-togethers, and other socials. Once, one of the horseshoes was somehow lost. We had several of the church people looking for it. We looked for it for several days but we could not find it. We were getting ready for a church social and needed the lost horseshoe. I decided to ask God to show us where that horseshoe was. I prayed, "Lord, I know You know where that horseshoe is. I also know You don't want us to spend more money for another set of horseshoes. So, please show me where to find that lost horseshoe." I left the church office, went out to the playground area, reached down into some weeds, and pulled out the 'lost' horseshoe. God knew where it was all the time!

On several occasions I have prayed for God to find us a parking place when the mall parking lot was full and there seemed to be no spaces available. My sister came to visit us from California. She did not believe in asking God for parking places. She was not physically well so I would pray, "God, we need a parking place near the entrance because Em is not able to walk very far." Every time I prayed such a prayer, we got just what we asked for! Often, it would be the closest one to the entrance. When she was preparing to leave to go back to California, she said, "When I get back home, I'm going to start praying for parking places!"

Once, I had looked for hours for my set of keys. I practically tore the house apart looking for those keys. Finally as a last resort, I asked God to find those keys for me. Immediately, I knew where they were. Sure enough, when I looked in that spot, the keys were there.

I have bothered Him with colds, headaches, and many other little things. He always hears the prayer offered in faith whether it is big or small. I learned God is God of the small things and He wants us to bring them to Him, too.

Jesus fed 5000 with "a few little fish."
(Matthew 15:24)
Elijah received an abundance of rain from "a little cloud." (I Kings 18:44)
The widow who fed Elijah had only a "little oil."
(I Kings 17:12)
The "little foxes" are said to destroy the nests.
(Song of Solomon 2:15)

IN THE NICK OF TIME
by Paul

We once read a verse somewhere in the *Living Bible* which read something like this, "God always acts in the nick of time." We have seen Him act on our behalf just at the right time on many occasions. One of these happened to an elderly woman who was a member of a church where I was pastor.

Mrs. G. lived alone. She had no children of her own but did have a niece whom she had reared after Mrs. G.'s sister had died. This niece did an excellent job of taking care of her. Since I was her pastor, I also tried to help look after her. She even gave me a key to her apartment so I would be able to get in if anything went wrong.

One day while I was having my prayer time, an urgency about Mrs. G. pressed on my mind. I had a very busy schedule that day so I thought, "I really must go see Mrs. G. tomorrow." However, the sense of urgency would not go away. In fact, the longer I waited the greater the urgency became. I busied myself doing all the trivial things I needed to do, but I couldn't get her off my mind. I finally decided to go see her. Since she only lived about five minutes from the church, it should take only a short time to drop by.

When I arrived at her house, I knocked loudly but there was no answer. I knocked again and again and still there was no answer. I was about to decide that she was not home. To make sure, I tried to look in the kitchen window but the drapes were closed and I couldn't see in. However,

I heard what sounded like a groan. I took the key she had given me and let myself in.

I found her semi-conscious, lying on the floor. She had had a light stroke and fallen. Immediately, I called the paramedics and her niece. By the time her niece arrived from work, the paramedics had her loaded into the ambulance and were headed for the hospital.

Later, I learned from her what had happened. After she had the stroke, she fell out of her bed and couldn't get up to reach the telephone. She had crawled, or scooted, out of the bedroom into the living room. She knew she needed help badly, but there was no way she could help herself. She began to pray for God to send her someone to help her. For some reason, she began to pray for God to send *me* to help her. Perhaps, she remembered that she had given me a key.

I don't know how the doctors calculated the time but they said if the medics had not arrived when they did, she would have been dead in a few short minutes. God heard her prayers and sent me to answer them just in the nick of time.

I learned from this incident, and many others, to act as quickly as possible on the prodding of the Holy Spirit. Someone's life may depend on what we do. He used me to bring a miracle to Mrs. G.

"There is an appointed time for everything, and there is a time for every event under heaven . . ."

(Ecclesiastes 3:1)

DON'T GIVE UP
ON THE BRINK OF A MIRACLE
by Alice

I've always loved music--many kinds of music--and I would have loved to sing or play an instrument. My dad had an old Zenith floor model radio with a speaker that could drive you out of the house. We listened to the Grand Ole Opry, the Hit Parade, gospel music, and the Old Fashioned Revival Hour. We listened, too! It wasn't just on in the background while we went about doing other things. Everybody got quiet and we stared at the radio like we stare at TV now. My dad and I listened to the arrangements and the instruments that were playing. I suppose we tried to imagine what all these entertainers looked like.

I would sing in our outside toilet. It became my auditorium where I pretended I was singing before large audiences. I belted out "Blue Moon Over My Shoulder" and "I'm Walking the Floor Over You," among other popular songs. I even learned to yodel some.

I really wanted to take piano lessons but we didn't have a piano. We lived with my grandparents and my granny made it quite clear that she didn't want to be bothered with the noise or the bulk of a piano. So that was that.

When I grew up and married a minister, I felt so handicapped because I could neither sing nor play a piano. Although ministers' wives may get by without singing, they always need to be able to play a piano.

My terrible fear of singing came in our rural two-room school when I was in first grade. We had assembly programs about once a month. This meant the heavy, wooden folding doors were opened and we could see the big kids and they could see us. If you could sing, tell a story or read a poem, you could have a part on the program. My talent was singing a little ditty of a song that began with "I've got rings on my fingers, bells on my toes . . . I'm a rinkdom, dinkdom, jittyboo jay." Silly song, but as a first grader, I could stand up there in front of everyone and belt it out. One day, I looked back and saw some of the older kids snickering. I though they were laughing at me. I was too little to understand that people laugh when little kids get up to perform and I was singing a very silly song. The laughing clicked in and I froze. I lost my nerve, never to regain it. As an adult, I wasn't even comfortable singing in the choirs in the churches where Paul was pastor.

Nearly 50 years later, an anointed singer, Mike Adkins, came to our church in Mount Sterling, and put on a wonderful concert. After the concert was over, I was looking around the table where he had records, books, and T-shirts for sale. My eyes fell on a tape of his music that wasn't just a tape: it was a soundtrack of the background music of his song, "Don't Give Up On The Brink of a Miracle." I bought it and began to play it in the car. I sang along with the tape until I finally got the courage to sing it in front of my family. They encouraged me to sing in church. Me, sing in church? By myself? After nearly 50 years? I sang, and since that time I have sung many times.

The miracle here, as I often tell the listeners, is not necessarily in my ability to sing but in the fact that I am standing in front of them singing.

What miracle are you waiting for? Don't wait 50 years

to let it happen. You could be on the brink of your miracle, you know.

"Be anxious for nothing, but in everything by prayer and supplication with thanksgiving let your requests be made known to God."

(Philippians 4:6)

SAVED FROM INJURIES
by Paul

During the months in which we were building our building, there were many opportunities for serious injuries. When we were laying the blocks for the basement wall, one man inadvertently stepped backward and fell approximately 8 feet onto some concrete blocks and other building materials. He got up, shook himself, and went back to work. Amazingly, he was not injured---not a scratch.

I, also, had some narrow escapes. One day I was putting 4'x8' sheets of Celotex on the outside of the building. I put up one sheet that had to be measured and sawed to fit into a corner about 20 feet from the ground. I went down off the ladder, measured and sawed the sheet to fit, carried it back up the ladder, and nailed it in place. While I was on the ladder, I wanted to take a good look to see if it fit properly. I momentarily forgot where I was and took a step backward. Of course, I fell off the ladder onto the very hard ground 20 feet below. Normally, a fall like this could injure one very seriously. I was stunned for a few seconds.

Then, I got up, checked for broken bones, moved around considerably, looked over the situation, and went back to work completely persuaded that God had broken my fall and kept me from a serious injury.

On another day when I was nailing materials to the 2'x4's, I hit my thumb with the hammer. It hurt very badly. Immediately, I cried out to Jesus and said, "Oh, Lord, heal me!" The pain subsided at once but my thumb was red all over. Looking at it from a purely human standpoint, it looked like I would lose my thumbnail and my thumb would be black and blue. However, that thumb never showed any effects whatever.

Looking back, it seems I tried my hand at everything that needed to be done. I even tried to drive the land moving equipment. We had a large pile of dirt that had been there for a long time and needed to be moved. I decided to drive the front-end loader and move it. I had driven a tractor which made driving the loader look easy. Therefore, I climbed on the tractor with the front-end loader on it, started it up, put the loader down on the ground, revved up the engine, and headed for that pile of dirt. The loader was supposed to go into the dirt and fill up. However, I failed to notice that the dirt was as hard as concrete. So, instead of the loader digging into the dirt, it started to move up the pile until it was about to flip the front of the tractor back over on me. Being a novice front-end-loader driver, I was helpless. "Help me, Jesus," I cried out. Immediately, my foot hit the clutch, even though at that instant I did not know where it was. This disengaged the gears and the tractor rolled back down the mound of dirt. I knew God had saved me once again.

I learned that God watches over His children to protect them, even when they don't know what they are doing.

"For it is thou who dost bless the righteous man, O Lord; thou dost surround him with favor as a shield."

(Psalm 5:12)

THE BOOK GETS PUBLISHED
By Paul

We started writing this book believing that God had commissioned us to tell the miracle stories which we have included herein. We felt God had anointed us for this project. Included in this was the desire to accomplish this by faith.

Soon after we made this project known to people in our church and other friends, the money to publish it began to come in from diverse sources. One of the men put a $100 bill in my hand during a church service and said, "This is for your book." Another man gave me a check for $500 and said the same thing.

During this period I was ministering to a family whose husband and father had cancer. To help with the family finances, his wife was baking bread in her home and selling it to raise money for their expenses. She felt led to give her tithe off this project toward the publishing of the book.

I went to a rural church to bring a message which I felt God had given me to share with the churches and a man gave me a check for $250.

Money came in the mail from people we did not know very well. Others gave us money which we felt they really couldn't afford. I went to get my hair cut---the barber gave me $100.

The point at which we really knew God was in this endeavor was on a Wednesday night. A woman came by the house after church and gave us a check for $1000. We were overwhelmed.

Other remarkable things have happened, too. I went to Walmart one day and two women gave me an envelope with $100 in it, $50 from each of them. On another occasion, we were driving on the local highway by-pass when a man flagged me down to give me $500. Deuteronomy 28:2 came to our minds, "And all these blessings shall come upon you and overtake you, if you will obey the Lord your God." This has always meant to me that God will chase you down in order to bless you.

One day at church a little 8 year old boy handed me an envelope with $10 in it. It was money he had earned from mowing lawns. This was a very touching experience.

All of these incidents brought in about three fifths of the money we needed. I could see God's hand moving but He was not moving fast enough for me. I began to think about ways I could raise the rest of the money. I decided to write all my friends, tell them what we were doing, and ask for a donation. I composed a money-raising letter to send.

When Alice came home from work that day, I read her my beautiful composition. She burst my bubble immediately when she said, "I thought we were going to do this by faith." I decided she was right, but I sent out one or two of these letters anyway. I received $10 from the people I had sent letters. I knew I had missed God, so I destroyed the rest of the letters.

Alice said several times, "I believe the money will come in many unexpected ways." So, we again renewed our faith that God was going to provide the money.

One day I talked to an old friend who told me about some good fortune he had by investigating an old annuity he had been in several years before. I, too, had been in an annuity program when I was a Southern Baptist. After I had drawn out all I had coming to me at the time, I was told when I reached 65 I would be able to draw $10 a month for the rest of my life. When I called to see if I could get my money now, they told me I had a total of $287 coming and they would send it to me in a few days. When it didn't come, I called back. I was told they had looked into my account and found I had "a good deal more" money due me. Well, as it turned out, I had enough in my account to finish paying for the book, to pay off all our debts and have some left over.

I learned again from this that God knows what we need before we ask. In fact, God knew twenty or thirty years ago that I would need that money to pay for a book we would write in 1995. It seems to me He had been keeping in store for me what we needed at this time. I am so glad He did!

"And my God shall supply all your needs according to His riches in glory in Christ Jesus."

(Phillipians 4:19)

Having read their story, if you wish to contact L.Paul and Alice Prather, you may reach them at:

P. O. Box 291,
Mt. Sterling, Kentucky 40353-0291
(606) 498-6191

Impac **Chris** **ian** **Books**

332 Leffingwell Ave., Suite 101
Kirkwood, MO 63122

AVAILABLE AT YOUR LOCAL BOOKSTORE, OR YOU MAY
ORDER DIRECTLY. Toll-Free, order-line only M/C, DISC,
or VISA 1-800-451-2708.

Write for *FREE* Catalog.